Provincial Archives of New Brunswick

''Mad Mizzie'', a local character and the only
survivor of a Scottish settlement near Stanley. She
made and sold brooms around the Nashwaak and
Miramichi.

Will O' The Wisp
FOLK TALES AND
LEGENDS OF NEW BRUNSWICK

brunswick press

Will O' The Wisp

FOLK TALES AND LEGENDS OF NEW BRUNSWICK

by Carole Spray

Brunswick Press
Fredericton, New Brunswick

Printed by Unipress
Fredericton, New Brunswick

1st printing — October 1979
2nd printing — November 1979
3rd printing — December 1979
4th printing — January 1980

The publisher thanks the Department of Youth, Recreation and Cultural Resources of New Brunswick for assistance in publishing this book.

Cover Photo by Freeman Patterson Courtesy of New Brunswick Department of Tourism

Canadian Cataloguing in Publication Data

Spray, Carole, 1942

Will O' the Wisp
ISBN 0 88790 106 9 pa.

1. Folklore — Atlantic Provinces. I. Title.
II. Title: Folk tales and legends of New Brunswick

GR113.566   398'.09715   C79-094373-5

Contents

In loving memory of Dr. Louise Manny
whose interest in folklore
inspired this book.

An evening at a lumber camp.

Preface

When Carole Spray asked me to write a preface to her collection of New Brunswick folktales, I was happy to accept. It meant that I would be one of the first to read the stories which I had been hearing about since she began recording them four years ago. A few folktales from New Brunswick have been published here and there in English (the Acadians have been more conscientious in documenting their oral culture) but this is the first extensive collection. I was eager to see what she had found.

Ms. Spray describes the first task faced by the student of folk narrative — collecting the tales — in her introduction. Once the neophyte collector gets over buck fever, hunting for story-tellers and recording their narratives are the most enjoyable parts of the whole process. By contrast, putting these essentially oral forms into writing is hard and tedious work. It is virtually impossible to capture the ambience of the storytelling event. The personalities of teller and audience, which shape the narrative anew each telling, are difficult to describe. The language used is essential to the art, but its pauses and repetitions look odd when pinned down in print. The place in which it is told, and the social and conversational events which precede and follow it — these too shape the story. Telling a tall tale on the Miramichi (or anywhere else in the province, for that matter) is the same kind of art that building a trap skiff is in Newfoundland outports. The patterns are passed on from one generation to the next, but no single telling (nor trap skiff) is the same as any other.

This is what makes the scholarly study of folktales such an interesting pursuit. Versions of the third story in this book have been collected throughout Europe as well as in India, Africa and the Americas. Yet this version has a special feature: when performed, the narrative is a *cante fable,* a combination of song and story. Ti-Jean feigns insanity in this version by singing a non-sensical song; in most versions he merely baas like a sheep.

Other kinds of variation are illustrated by the story "Up A Tree" in the section on yarns and tall tales. For one thing, it has become localized. Other North American versions of this tall tale involve wolves rather than the moose depicted in this New Brunswick version. It has also been given a unique topical ending, typical of the accretions which folk narratives gather as story tellers tailor them to fit contemporary audiences.

Folk narratives are at once universal and specially adapted to the circumstances of each telling. They not only entertain but educate, expressing the ideals and describing the cultural patterns of those who tell and listen to them. For example, legends, "true" stories about real people and events, are inextricably woven into patterns of belief and practice. The plots of such narratives vary considerably from one community to the next even when the underlying belief remains the same.

In Chipman, N.B., I recorded a story about a "wicked man" on the Salmon River who captured those easily tamed birds, gorbeys (Canada Jays), held them down with a forked stick, and set fire to them. One night his camp caught fire, he hit his head on a low beam trying to get out the door, fell back and was badly burned. He carried the marks of this for the rest of his life. In the words of the man who told me of the happening, "they credited his disaster with cruelty," for everyone knows that it is bad luck to harm a gorbey. "The Man Who Plucked the Gorbey" in this collection elaborates upon the same theme, but gives a completely different set of details. These stories share not just a belief about luck and gorbies but also a more general belief that disaster awaits those who knowingly tempt fate through the flagrant disregard of accepted beliefs and practices.

Every story in this collection could be analyzed in terms of its cultural significance and the variations in style and content which it represents. I am happy that the Memorial University of Newfoundland Folklore and Language Archive was allowed to make copies of Ms. Spray's original recordings, for hers is an excellent collection, with lasting value to scholars interested in such analysis. But it is appropriate that Ms. Spray has chosen to present them in the format of a book for the general public, because they are fascinating and entertaining documents of an aspect of New Brunswick's culture which is basic but ephemeral. Her introductory comments remind us that folk narratives belong to the present as well as the past, can be found in every age group, and are part of urban as well as rural existence. Story-telling is a special art, but there are specialists of this sort in virtually every community. Readers of this book who have spent any amount of time in New Brunswick will find some familiar stories. New Brunswick's folk traditions are worth learning about; I hope the publication of these stories will encourage others to collect and study them.

Neil V. Rosenberg
Director
Memorial University of
  Newfoundland Folklore and
  Language Archive

Acknowledgements

Several people helped in preparing this book. My husband Bill gave me much support and encouragement. He read the manuscript several times, helped with the typing, and his ideas, criticism and thorough knowledge of New Brunswick history were invaluable.

Edith Butler and Ken Homer graciously gave their permission to use *Do You Want to Buy a Cow?* and *Will O' the Wisp*. Professor Edward D. (Sandy) Ives of the University of Maine gave me permission to use material from the Northeast Archives of Folklore and Oral History and both he and his wife Bobby were very kind to me when I visited Orono. Professor Neil Rosenberg of Memorial University of Newfoundland provided reading lists to help answer my questions about folklore. Mary Flagg helped me locate material in the Archives of the Harriet Irving Library and the staff at the Provincial Archives and the Legislative Library were also very helpful. The Explorations Program of the Canada Council provided financial assistance which made it possible for me to collect the stories. All the people I interviewed were generous with their time, told fascinating tales, and were most hospitable.

Thank you very much.

Collecting the Stories

I must confess that on the day in 1966 when Dr. Louise Manny tried to persuade me to attend the Miramichi Folksong Festival in Newcastle, I made excuses. I'd heard some of the songs on the radio that afternoon and I didn't feel too keen about attending a live performance. The truth is, I was used to the more conventional modern and classical music and folksongs sounded uninteresting to me. As for folktales, I thought I could learn everything there was to know by reading English literature. Being a true New Brunswicker, I felt sure that if there was folklore around here, it probably wasn't significant, and if it was significant, then there wouldn't be much of it in New Brunswick anyway. All of which shows that I knew absolutely nothing about folklore and even less about New Brunswick, although I had lived here all my life.

But I never forgot Dr. Manny. She was the founder of the Miramichi Folksong Festival, author of *Ships of Miramichi,* and co-author with James Wilson of the classic *Folksongs of Miramichi.* Her accomplishments and her great personal vitality and integrity inspired both love and respect. After she died, the thought kept nagging at me that if New Brunswick folklore was important to her, then there must be something in it. Many of the songs had been collected, but I remembered her saying "There are lots of good stories here". I wondered, what kind of stories might they be? And how could I collect them?

Of course, professional folklorists like Marius Barbeau and Helen Creighton had collected material in New Brunswick for years and this is continued today by Edward D. (Sandy) Ives, Neil Rosenberg, Sister Catherine Jolicoeur and Charlotte Cormier, to name a few. The songs are not neglected; there are *Folksongs of Miramichi,* Creighton's *Folksongs from Southern New Brunswick,* and if you can obtain a copy of Edward D.

(Sandy) Ives's book on *Joe Scott,* the songmaker from Lower Woodstock, you'll be very lucky indeed. But there are few books available in English which deal directly with the subject of legends and folktales with an emphasis on New Brunswick.

What is folklore anyway? I wasn't sure what I was searching for and when I consulted the *Standard Dictionary of Folklore,* I found twenty-three separate definitions and that confused me even more. Folklorists themselves can't seem to agree on any one in particular, but, I think we can say that folklore is almost any tradition or expression that is circulated informally among members of a group. It includes songs, stories, sayings, superstitions and recitations. Often the author is unknown and usually there is more than one version.

I began to listen and to talk to people about local folklore and I poked through material in libraries and archives for evidence of tales that had been collected in the past. I found Dr. Manny was right. "There are lots of good stories here." To properly research and collect these stories, I knew I would need a tape recorder, a baby-sitter, and lots of gas. Fortunately, the Canada Council provided me with an Explorations grant, and I was "off-and-running".

I started with my relatives. I was delighted to hear my father, Edward Jeffrey, telling stories I'd heard as a child; stories I had almost forgotten. He told me about a man who found Acadian gold in the bank of the Memramcook River, about the treasure supposedly buried under the old Fitzsimmons Reservoir in Moncton, and about the ghost who haunted his old home on Lester Avenue. The ghost wore a bowler hat, a high-winged collar and a coat with split tails. He used to walk out of one of the bedrooms, and down the stairs. His footsteps could be heard and whenever he appeared, you could see right through him. It turned out that the main structure of the old house had once been a barn and a man who faced financial ruin hanged himself from the rafters.

I discovered that my father-in-law had heard about the ghost of an old sea captain who died of the fever back in the days when Irish immigrants landed on Sheldrake Island. The wife of a lighthouse keeper used to see the apparition roaming up and down the shore. He told me how the organ in his house began playing at the very moment when a neighbour killed herself. I learned about the headless nun who haunts Morrison Cove Bridge, and I listened to tall tales about how large the mosquitoes were and how thick the fog was around Miramichi Bay.

After I had exhausted my relatives, I started working on friends and acquaintances. I soon learned that it was pointless to ask "Do you know any folklore?" because most people said "No", but if I said "Do you know any stories or superstitions or cures?", then usually I'd get "Yes" for an answer. A lot of people could think of someone else who knew stories too, and soon I had a long list of people to interview. If I didn't know a person, I'd write a letter to them explaining what I was up to, followed by a phone call and then a visit. Sometimes just a visit would do. In the beginning, I thought it would take three or four sessions before anyone could relax enough to face a microphone. But it didn't turn out that way. With few exceptions, people opened up within the first hour and became so engrossed in the stories they were telling or the songs they were singing that all self-consciousness seemed to disappear.

The first real stranger I interviewed was Harding Smith, an 87 year old lumberman who lived in Fredericton but had spent much of his life around Parker's Ridge. "Smiddy" was eager to talk about the old days and to tell stories, and like many older people, his memory for the past was as sharp as a whetted knife. He sang more than twenty-eight songs for me, some of them with verses as long as your arm, and he told of his times in the lumber camps as if it had happened the day before. I saw him every week for over six months because his oral history of early days in New Brunswick was almost as fascinating as the man himself. I'll never forget visiting him in hospital a few days before he died. By then we had become firm friends, and as I sat on the edge of his bed he raised himself up on one elbow and began, "Say, did I ever tell you about Geordie Brown and the pancakes . . . . .?" He went on for almost an hour, laughing, talking and even singing, as if it were someone else who carried his pain and as if he had an eternity of bright tomorrows to live. "See ya," he said.

I spent a lot of time on Miramichi. The people are friendly and the area is uncommonly rich in folklore. Once I started in an area like that, I found it was hard to stop because one person led to another all up and down the river and some people became friends I visited more than once. Most of the stories in this area come from the lumber camps, and that's not surprising since a good proportion of the men who lived along the major waterways in this province made their living as lumbermen.

The men would go into the woods in the fall of the year, and not come out until spring. Living together in small isolated communities forced people to rely on themselves for nearly everything. The men sometimes conducted their own funerals, buried their companions in make-shift coffins such as a pork barrel or two flour barrels, and marked the place by nailing a shoepack to a tree at the head of the grave. They devised their own remedies, provided their own entertainments, and commemorated events by making up songs and poems and stories. They sang about the deaths of their comrades such as Peter Emberley and Samuel Allen, about the horrors of the Miramichi Fire and about the joys of Duffy's Hotel.

It was a tough life filled with danger and rewarded with very little pay. If a man wasn't killed by a falling log or washed away by floodwaters, he might slip into the river during a stream drive or take a fall while dislodging a tree. I heard about one foreman who carried a rifle with him on his rounds. When he saw one of his men twenty feet up trying to chop free a lodged tree he said, "If you don't come down I'll kill ya, 'cause I don't want no dead men around here!"

Dead Man Camp was the name given to one lumbering operation near Burnt Hill, New Brunswick. According to this story, a teamster arrived in camp late one night with his horses hauling a full load of logs. Because the road to the landing was very steep and treacherous, the boss told him "You'd better put your team away and wait until morning to unload". But the teamster was stubborn.

"I'll either land this load, or I'll eat my supper in hell," he said, and away he went as if the Devil himself was after him. The horses missed a sharp turn in the road, over-shot the landing and crashed into the river, killing all. The place is supposed to be haunted, and it is said that any team of horses will balk and refuse to proceed down that hill.

Like most of us, lumbermen relied on their own feelings about experience to interpret the cause and effect of events. They were naturally superstitious. It was believed you should never hire on a Friday because whoever was hired then wouldn't stay the whole season, and if a man got a chain knotted, it meant he would quit. A camp built of popple wood was bad luck because Christ's cross was made of popple. To sing the song "Peter Emberley" in camp meant that someone would get hurt. If a man slept with his head facing downstream he risked drowning and if he went to bed with his axe embedded in wood, he would get no sleep. Teamsters relied on this little ditty when they went to buy a horse:

4

One white foot, try him;
Two white feet, buy him;
Three white feet, deny him;
Four white feet and one white nose
Cut off his head and throw him to the crows.

On Saturday night and Sunday, the men had time off and then there'd be singing and dancing, fiddling and diddling, story-telling and games. Sometimes the games were invented by the men themselves or else they were adapted from games they had learned at home. They included *Hot-Ass, Jack-in-the-Dark, Rooster, Shoulder-the-Sheep, Selling-the-Salt and Shuffle-the-Brogue.* In the latter game, the men would sit in a circle around the person who was "It". A shoepack would be passed around under the men's knees. When "It" had his back turned, someone would hurl the shoepack at him and he had to guess who had thrown it. If he guessed correctly, that person became "It", but if he made a mistake, the game continued as before.

One of the most interesting games I heard about was "Uncle Allan's Rope Trick". Uncle Allan bored holes through a deacon's bench and threaded a rope through it every which way and then tied the rope in a knot. The men were supposed to figure out how to get the rope out of the deacon's bench without untying the knot. They worked at it all fall, winter, and spring without success. Before the camp broke up for the summer, one of the men came to Uncle Allan and said, "What's the secret of getting that rope out without untying the knot?" Uncle Allan's reply was: "The secret is, it can't be done". The important thing was to give the men something to do.

Like most legends and tales, the stories told by the men grew from their own experience or else they evolved from traditional stories, but regardless of the source, the stories would be expanded or changed a little with each telling. Over the years as the men moved from one camp or one place to another, they took their stories with them. That's why the legend *The Man Who Plucked the Gorbey* can be found throughout New Brunswick and Maine. Stories vaguely similar to some of those told about Will Lolar are also told in Maine about a character called George Knox who was supposedly in league with the Devil.

Other stories such as *Three Gold Hairs From the Giant's Back* were told not because they had anything to do with the lumber woods, but because of their entertainment value. These wonder tales or *"Marchen"* tell of giants and fairies and other magical beings, and they are quite rare. They come from many cultures and go back many generations, even beyond the Brothers Grimm who first collected these stories from the European oral tradition. *Three Hairs From the Giant's Back* has been collected before from Wilmot MacDonald by both Creighton and Ives. A verbatum transcript and a good discussion of the story appears in *Northeast Folklore,* Vol. IV.

In the past, self-reliance was a way of life not only in the lumber camps but also in the general community of the Maritimes. When people were sick, they often had no choice but to cure themselves. Some of the cures were unusual. If you had asthma the thing to do was to bore a hole in a tree at the exact height of your head. Then, cut off a lock of your hair, put it in the hole and plug the hole. By the time you grew past that hole in the tree you'd be cured. However, if you happened to be bald or finished growing, you could eat field mice fried in butter. Smelly socks tied around the neck, goose grease on the chest and salt fish bound onto the feet would cure a sore throat, cold and fever. For rheumatism or arthritis, you might put a piece of copper in your pocket or shoe and sleep with potatoes in your bed. The best thing for a sore back was to find someone who was born at Christmas and get them to walk up and down your spine. The following story illustrates just how effective some remedies could be:

> It was wintertime and this fella's wife had the earache awful bad. She was moanin' and groanin' and 'pon my soul it near killed her.
> So her husband said, "I'm gonna cure your earache."
> And she said, "How?"
> "Well," he said, "just you wait."
> He went out and he got a stick of white maplewood, and he stuck it in the oven with one end of it hanging down. After a while, the log began to thaw and sizzle and the hot sap began trickling out. The husband caught the sap in a teaspoon and went and poured it into her ear.
> Oh, it near burnt the head off a' her. She jumped out of bed hanging onto her ear with the most awfullest yowling you've ever heard.
> "My, my," he said. "I think the cure is worse than the disease."
> (Horace Hunter, Astle.)

Since doctors were scarce and home remedies often failed, people would call upon healers and charmers to cure certain ailments. Blood

6

Father William Morriscy, clairvoyant physician from Bartibogue.

charmers were common everywhere, but the secret of the charm itself was not easy to obtain. There are many variations of this procedure, but usually a man could tell one woman and a woman could tell one man, but if the rule wasn't followed, the power to charm blood was lost. The blood charmer would place one hand on the patient's head and the other hand on the wound. The patient had to speak his full name and then the charmer whispered some words from Ezekiel whereupon the blood clotted and the wound healed.

In 1881, the New Brunswick Medical Act was passed preventing anyone except licensed physicians to practice medicine, but this did not include "clairvoyant physicians practicing prior to 25th March 1881". The special status of "clairvoyant physician" applied to the Rev. Harry Price, a Presbyterian minister at Boiestown who was famous for setting bones and to Father William Morriscy of Bartibogue.

Father Morriscy was born in Halifax in 1841, and after studying medicine for two years, he trained for the priesthood at St. Michael's College, then served in Caraquet and Bathurst under Father Pacquet, a qualified physician. Probably Father Morriscy learned a lot from the older priest, but the young man possessed a rare gift. He had the uncanny ability to diagnose an illness simply by looking at the patient. By the time Father Morriscy became pastor at Bartibogue in 1877, he was widely known and people were travelling from the United States and from as far west as British Columbia to be cured by him. He used balsam and herbs and other natural ingredients in his remedies and they say much of his knowledge came to him from the Micmac tribe at Burnt Church.

According to legend, this priest's charity was unlimited. Never would he accept pay for his services and when one patient left a gold coin on his table, Father Morriscy hitched up his horse and galloped after him to return the money. Once in the midst of a violent storm, a call came to him from an ailing Protestant who had been abandoned and left to die. The priest knew from the description of the disease that the man couldn't be helped medically, and since he was not of the same faith the man didn't require spiritual assistance either. Nevertheless, Father Morriscy started out at five o'clock in the morning and after exhausting three horses, he arrived at the man's bedside at ten o'clock that night. The ailing Protestant died, but not uncomforted or alone.

Father Morriscy's work continued even after his death in 1908, for he left his prescriptions to the Sisters of the Hotel Dieu Hospital in Chatham. They possessed neither the way nor the means to place these remedies before the public and so a group of Moncton businessmen formed "The Father Morriscy Medicine Company", which later moved to Montreal. The cures were marketed far and wide and Father Morriscy of Bartibogue became famous all over North America. As a folk-hero, he has been remembered in a number of poems, and one of them entitled "A Christmas Greeting 1885" was written by Michael Whelan, the poet of Renous.

Father Ryan of Red Bank died only a few years ago, and he too was famous for his cures. One man told me of how he had frozen his hand when he fell through the ice and the doctor informed him that his fingers would have to be cut off. The man refused such drastic measures and went to Father Ryan for advice. The priest instructed him to soak his fingers in alcohol for an hour each day and put them in pickle brine three times a week. Today the man boasts that his hand is in perfect shape because of the priest's advice. Father Ryan's remedy for rashes was to boil straw in a bucket of water and then use the water for washing, but his favourite cure-all was to bathe in a tub filled with pine boughs and eggs, broken shells and all. According to local tradition, a famous country and western singer came to the priest with cancer of the throat. The man spent all of one summer at Red Bank, and Father Ryan is said to have cured him so completely that he is still a top singing star today.

I doubt that Father Ryan ever pretended to be a licensed physician, but people sought comfort from him and believed in him and like the good Bishop in the tale, *The Woman, the Bishop and the Cow,* he did what he could. The patient's improved state of mind was perhaps almost as important in bringing about a cure as the remedy itself. Time and faith were as potent then as they are now.

The stories told about Father Delagarde at New Mills and Benjamin River are almost all examples of faith healing. Many speak with great awe and admiration of this strict but beloved priest. He served the people in this area for almost twenty-five years and when his parishioners called on him, he prayed from his book, laid his hands upon them and gave firm but gentle words of encouragement. His parishioners tell how he cured one woman dying of tuberculosis so that she lived to raise her many children. They say that a baby who was dying of fever recovered after Father Delagarde prayed over him, and an older child recovered from what was thought to be a case of spinal meningitis. His people speak of him as a "holy priest" and he was buried about twenty years ago near the place where he was born, in St. Isadore, Gloucester County.

As far as I know, neither Father Ryan nor Father Delagarde were remembered in song or verse as were some local heroes. Many of the poems I collected were written, like the songs, about murder, shipwrecks and death or else they were satires on local characters and events. Usually these verses were simply committed to memory, but occasionally broadsheets were printed and sold in the streets. For instance, in Saint John, a British spectator wrote an epic poem entitled "The Race and the Death of John Renforth" which was sold in the streets in 1871. It concerned the famous boatrace between "the Tyne Crew" of England and four men of Saint John, who made up "the Paris Crew". John Renforth was the stroke of the British team and he died of a heart attack in a last desperate attempt to overtake the Paris Crew. The Saint John team won and the poet made enough money from his verse to pay his passage home to England.

The famous Bannister Murder which occurred near Moncton in the 1930's inspired a poem called "The Pacific Junction Tragedy". It was written by C.H. Murray and sold in the streets of Moncton for fifteen cents a copy. Part of it went:

> *The day of execution came*
> *It was an awful sight*
> *To see those poor brothers*
> *Marching in the morning light.*
>
> *And one spoke to the hangman*
> *These words they heard him say*
> *"The rope is choking me", he said*
> *"And I would like to pray."*

Some verses were, and still are, recited at concerts and community entertainments. Among the most popular at Miramichi are Hedley Parker's "The Days of Duffy Gillis" and "The Man Behind the Boathook" about early lumbering days and the breaking of the South West Boom. Another common favourite is James Hannay's "The Maiden's Sacrifice", and equally interesting as a recitation is "The Ballad of Margery Grey", a sad lament about a woman with a baby who wanders from the family homestead and perishes in the snow. Some of the recitations came from old school texts and were learned in the era when schools put more emphasis on memory. Others come from anonymous or uncertain sources, such as this saga which Carl Webber of Chipman recites about a man who had twenty-eight names.

The Fella With Twenty-Eight Names

> *I was brought to be christened before I could speak*
> *So I cannot account for this terrible freak*
> *My mother and father were excellent folk*
> *So when I was born they were both of one mind*
> *And they said, "Let us give him all the names we can find."*
> *And so they consented as wise as could be*
> *And this is the handle they stuck unto me:*
> *Jonathan, Joseph, Jeremiah,*
> *Timothy, Titus, Obediah,*
> *William, Walker, Henry, Sim,*
> *Reuben, Rufus, Solomon, Jim,*
> *Nathaniel, Daniel, Abraham,*
> *Roderick, Frederick, Peter and Sam,*

Hiram, Tyler, Nicholas, Pat,
Christopher, Dib, Jehosophat,

When I went and got married, the case was so bad
The preacher looked at me as if I were mad
Said he, "Young man, it is a great shame
Your parents denied you a sensible name.
Say nothing more, but for reasons of mine,
You will have to be married a bit at a time."
Jonathan, Joseph . . . . . . (repeat all names)

When I joined the club, the clerk of the town was
* calling the roll,*
And he ended with my name. And there wasn't a soul
To wait for the end. They all got so vexed,
They said they'd go home, and come back for the rest.

Of course, recitations don't have to rhyme. Some were simply pieces of nonsense prose like this one:

A boy lost about the size of man. He was barefooted with his father's shoes on. He was born before his eldest brother and his mother was absent at the occasion. His hair was cut curly and he was cross-eyed at the back of his neck. He had on a mutton-chop coat with bean soup lining. He had on his back an empty sack containing two railroad tongues and three bung holes. The last place he was seen was on the courthouse roof shovelling wind. Anybody knowing his whereabouts, please notify his Aunt Ruth. (Carl Webber, Chipman)

Another kind of folk poetry is the jump-rope rhyme heard on sidewalks and in schoolyards, and it provides interesting insights into how children view the world. The simplest is a "plain jump-rhyme" in which the child skips to the rhythms of the verse. This one came from Kathy McDonnell of St. Dunstan's School in Fredericton.

Miss Monroe
Broke her toe
Riding on a buffalo
The buffalo died
And Miss Munroe cried
And that's the end of the buffalo ride.

The endurance or "prophetic" rhymes are more complicated, and they can be quite grisly.

> *Fudge, Fudge, call the judge*
> *Jane is gonna have a baby*
> *Jack is going crazy*
> *Boy, Girl, Boy, Girl . . .(skip until miss to tell which gender)*
> *Wrap it up in tissue paper*
> *Send it down the elevator*
> *One, two, three, four . . . . (skip until miss to tell how many chil-*
> *   dren)*

Children are excellent sources of folklore. Maybe that's because they are generally receptive and more open to imaginative pursuits, and both playgrounds and schoolyards provide group situations where traditions can be passed on informally. Elementary school children love to tell "Shaggy Dog Stories" which go on and on and carry a strong punch line as in *The Ghost of the One Black Eye.* And then there are the jokes about the "little moron" or the "Newfie" or yet another variation on the "Knock-Knock" theme which is so common.

Riddles are very popular, especially among pre-schoolers who tend to ask the same riddle of the same person over and over again. I wonder if this is because young children are especially tickled by this brand of humour or because they take delight in practicing a new skill or because "one-up-manship" over anyone is a new and pleasant experience.

Superstition in children begins very early, as soon as they begin to notice cause and effect. Whenever the car is stopped at a red light, our children love to chant, "Red, red, turn to green". When the inevitable happens and the light changes, they seem enormously pleased with themselves. It's not that they don't understand that stop-lights work by electricity, they just prefer to believe in their own power to influence events. Almost every child knows the old saying "Step on a crack, you'll break your mother's back", and I've seen children as young as three and four go out of their way to avoid walking on cracks in the sidewalk. It is a rudimentary game which coincides with the development of conscience.

The concerns of older children are often expressed in certain folk practices. For instance, a young girl might try to find out who her future husband will be by peeling an apple and throwing the peel over her shoulder. If it falls in the shape of a letter, then that letter signifies the first letter in her future husband's name. Teenagers may try to "raise the Devil" in more ways than one. One method is to read the Lord's Prayer backwards. Another is to go down cellar and walk around counter-clockwise with a white candle seven times. Then, if you look in a mirror, you'll see the Devil over your left shoulder. I've heard plenty about this practice, but nothing about the results!

Although most teenagers possess a keen interest in the supernatural, all of the "serious" ghost stories I collected came from older people, the youngest of whom was in his mid-twenties. In a way, ghost stories were one of the most touchy areas of belief because many of the people who told these stories were firmly convinced of their reality, and were most anxious for me to believe so too. Personally, I find it very easy to suspend disbelief with even the wildest of tales and I found some of these stories sounded very convincing. I've never seen a ghost myself, but I firmly believe these things do occur. The explanation is beyond me.

Despite the sensitivity felt towards ghost stories and certain beliefs, almost everybody I met was willing to take the time to think of stories, songs, superstitions and cures. Even though I was a complete stranger, people showed me around their community, introduced me to their friends and invited me into their homes. This sort of consideration was shown not only by country people but by 'city folk' as well. When I visited the Northeast Archives of Folklore and Oral History the hospitality of Sandy Ives and his wife Bobby went far beyond the call of duty. When I travelled to the Amos farmhouse in McNairn Settlement, Kent County, I was greeted with a hot cup of tea, a warm supper and stories that went on non-stop well past midnight. I got up early next morning, and I found Mr. Amos waiting for me with his chair pulled up, his arms folded and his eyes on the tape-recorder. "Plug that thing in," he said, "and let's get going."

Of course there were problems. There was the time I travelled fifty miles, twice, to interview an old fellow who turned out to be mike-shy. "He's hiding in the woodshed," said his wife. But all I got to see was a patch of blue shirt disappearing through the bushes up Porter Cove Brook. And then there was the time the car engine caught fire, sending up ominous billows of smoke. I stood alone on the side of the road in the pouring rain, laden with suitcases, camera, tape-recorder and unsuitably dressed for the occasion. Fortunately I was on the main highway, and hailed a bus to get back home.

Another problem was the one I faced when I had to turn the transcriptions from tape into general reading material. My ideal was to tell the tales exactly as they were told. I soon found out it couldn't be done because it was impossible to capture in print the facial expressions, the gestures and cadence of voice of a master story-teller. Good story-tellers will back-track, digress and speak in sentence fragments, all of which is natural and entertaining. It adds to the live performance and it sounds great. But if you try to transfer the same thing into print, it doesn't read well. Occasionally I had to interfere with story progression, sentence structures and phrasing while maintaining the tone, rhythms, speech patterns and, of course, the story line given by the actual narrator. Wherever possible, I used the speech idioms of the storyteller himself to convey the distinctive poetry of common language.

Some of the stories were told by two people at once (such as the Estey brothers who told *The Red Haired Girl*) and other times three or four people told me different anecdotes which centred around one theme, as in the Gorbey story and *The Wizard of Miramichi*. I found it awkward to try to maintain more than one or two narrators at once and so I solved the problem by keeping the tone but using my own "voice". I also did this when I adapted stories from a printed source. And so, there are a variety of styles here, and perhaps that is as it should be.

It was great fun. I discovered that folklore is not something which occupies a dusty corner in a backroom of the far distant past. It's an on-going process. Young anglers and hunters still tell tall tales and yarns and no doubt in the future those stories will be lengthened or widened or changed some way. And, when somebody sees a fire-ball today, they might not think of "Will O' the Wisp" or "feu follet", but they may believe they have seen a U.F.O. or flying saucer, because the unknown must always be explained, one way or another. That's part of the myth-making process.

True, stories like those told about Geordie Brown come from a bygone age, as do the stories told about other characters like "Snake-eye Jim" who was so long and skinny it took him half an hour to uncoil; or Father Savage of Moncton who, when a fat lady waddled to the front of his church in the middle of mass, said "We will be silent and wait for the Queen Mary to dock"; or Charlie Cahill of Juniper who hung a big sign by the highway which read, "SEE THE IRON SPRING", and then lured curious tourists into the woods to see a rusty bed-spring hanging from a tree. But, wherever there are characters and topical local events, people will remember them to a certain extent in stories or in songs or in verse. Whenever there is mystery or uncertainty, people will provide their own solutions, especially where none other exists; and ghost stories will be with us for as long as ghosts are seen.

Folklore will be found wherever there are folks.

A tintype of Gabe Acquin, taken during his visit to England.

Folk Tales and Legends

15

Will O'The Wisp

Many people in the Atlantic region of Canada are familiar with marsh fires and many stories of the supernatural are told concerning this phenomenon. It is sometimes called "Will O' the Wisp" or "Jack O' Lantern," but the Acadians refer to it as "feu follet" (or dancing lights) and it was believed that a sorcerer could change his body into the shape of a "feu follet" and follow people around. The solution to the problem was to stick a knife into a tree stump and say, "I command you to pass under the point of that knife." The fire would then disappear, leaving only a spatter of blood on the tree stump. The Malecite Indians call the fire balls "Esk-wid-eh-wid" and they are believed to be a forerunner of death.

The story of Will O' the Wisp is an attempt to explain the origin of these fires which lurk near wet and swampy areas and which scare the unsuspecting wanderer half-to-death. Ken Homer of Woodstock collected this story from Allie Sweeney of Digby, Nova Scotia. The tape is deposited in the Northeast Archives of Folklore and Oral History at the University of Maine.

There once was a blacksmith by the name of Willy O'Connor who came to this country from Ireland many years ago. He settled down in the Maritimes and tried to make a living for himself by shoeing horses and mending iron. Money was pretty scarce in those days and he could never earn enough to keep himself and his family in comfort. He worked day and night over the hot forge, with his muscles straining, and the sweat pouring from his brow. But nothing changed. He remained poor.

One morning when there was not even enough oatmeal to fill his belly, Willy got very angry. He shook his fists and said,

"Begorra! I swear that if the Devil came along I'd sell myself to him just for the money."

As he started off for work that morning, he met a tall skinny man in a big high hat with a black horse.

"Good morning to you, Willie."

Willie looked at him closely. He had never seen the likes of him before.

"I don't know you," said Willie.

"Well," said the stranger, "I know you. And I heard you talking this

16

very morning about how you'd sell yourself to the Devil if he came along. Here's your big chance. I am the Devil."

For a minute, Willie didn't know what to say. He was pretty scared.

"Tell you what," said the Devil, "I'll make a bargain with you. I'll give you all the money you can spend for seven years, and after the seven years are up, I'll come and get you."

Willie thought about it and he figured that seven years was quite a long while, so he decided to make the bargain.

Oh, it was grand! There wasn't a thing in the world he couldn't buy if he wanted it, and he bought just about everything in the world he wanted. He got a new house, new clothes, new horses, new wagons and even a new shillelagh. And, just to show he wasn't a bit mean, he built new churches and schools and he always helped the poor.

One day, an old man came to his door. All dressed in rags he was, and very tired and hungry with not a penny of his own to buy food.

"Come in," said Willie. "Sit down. Stay for dinner."

So, the man stayed and shared Willie's dinner. He came in the next day and shared his dinner and on the third day too. Finally, the old man said,

"Willie, you've been good to me. If there's anything you'd like to wish for, I have the power to grant you three wishes, because I am an angel."

"Really?" said Willie. "Is that a fact? Well, if that's the case then, I wish for a chair that whoever sits in it can't get out till I say so. And I wish for an anvil, that whoever hangs onto it can't let go till I release them. And, I wish for a steel purse so that whatever I put into it can't get out until I decide to take it out."

"Your wishes are granted," said the angel. And he disappeared.

Seven years went by in no time at all, and of course the Devil came as he promised he would. Willie was shaving himself when the knock came on his door.

"Willie, it's me. The Devil. I'm after you."

"So I see," said Willie. "Tell you what, Devil, you just sit yourself down in that chair while I finish shaving. I want to look my best if I'm going along with you."

So, the Devil sat in the chair. But, when he tried to stand up again, he couldn't get out of it. He was stuck.

"A-ha!" said Willie. "Now I've got you just where I want you. And he went and he got a big iron pipe and began pounding the Devil with it.

"Ouch! Stop! Let me go," hollared the Devil. "Let me go and I'll give you seven more years and all the money you can spend."

"It's a deal," said Willie. And he let the Devil loose.

The next seven years went just as quickly as the first. Willie had a lovely time spending his money, but, all too soon, the Devil was at his door again.

Knock. Knock.

"Who's there?" asked Willie.

"It's the Devil."

"Well, come on in, Devil. Will you hang onto this anvil for me while I go and fetch my hat?"

"Certainly! Anything to oblige!"

So Willie went upstairs, but he didn't get his hat. Instead, he came back with his big, iron bar. When the Devil saw that, he tried to let go of the anvil and run, but he couldn't. His hands stuck right to it. Well, the Devil took a terrible beating just like he did before. He couldn't stand much of that, so he promised Willie another seven years and all the money he could spend. Naturally, Willie agreed to let him go.

Things went pretty well until the seven years passed and then, it was Devil-time again. On this occasion, the Devil walked right into the blacksmith shop, grabbed Willie by the collar, and said,

"OK, Willie. Now I've got you. No tricks this time. You're coming along with me."

"Well," said Willie, "I suppose I'll have to go."

So, he and the Devil took off down the road. They were going by a bar-room when Willie sighed and said, "You know, Devil, it's the first time in many years that I've passed by this place and not had the price of a drink in my pocket. I sure could use a drink because the place we're going to is certain to be very, very hot."

The Devil felt kind of sorry for Willie and he said, "I'll turn myself into a piece of silver so that you can buy yourself a drink."

Well, when the Devil did that, Willie grabbed the silver coin. He fastened it in his purse, ran back to the blacksmith shop and threw the purse into the fire.

The Devil began to hollar,

"Oh, help! Let me out. I can't stand this kind of punishment Willie. Let me out!"

But Willie got hold of his bellows and kept pumping and blowing at the fire until the steel purse was so hot it almost melted. Then he took it out, put it on his anvil and pounded away at it, then put it back in the fire, and then pounded it some more.

The pain was something fierce, and the poor Devil could stand it no longer.

"Willie, let me out, and I'll never bother you again."

So, Willie took him out of the purse, cooled him off, and let him go. And true to his word, the Devil never bothered Willie again as long as he lived. But, soon, Willie got to be an old man. Then he died and took off for heaven.

Knock. Knock.

"Who's that?" said Saint Peter.

"It's me. Willie O'Connor."

"Oh. So, it's you, is it. Well, I'm sorry but I can't let you in. One of our angels gave you three chances to get in here. You didn't wish for it then, and it's too late now. Good-bye!" and he slammed the pearly gates right in Willie's face.

Poor Willie. There was no place for him to go now except down to the other place where the Devil lived. So, down he went and knocked on the gate.

"Who's there?" shouted the Devil.

"It's your friend, Willie O'Connor."

"Heaven help us!", cried the Devil. "You can't come in here. I've had enough trouble from you Willie O'Connor, and I don't want any more. Go away!"

"But, I have nowhere to go," said Willie. "They won't let me into heaven, and now you say I can't come down here. What am I supposed to do?"

The Devil decided he'd better try to help him out. So, he reached inside his door, lit one of his straw wisps and handed it to Willie.

"I won't have the likes of you in here, but you can go to work for me out in the world. You take this fiery wisp, and wherever you find people who are silly from drinking too much, get them to follow your light into the water and let them drown. I'll use them for firewood."

And Willie did.

If ever you see a wisp of fire wandering near the water or marshland, you'll know who it is. It's just Willie O'Connor, more commonly known as Will O' the Wisp.

The Woman, the Bishop
and the Cow

I heard this story in 1976 from Ralph Amos who was keeper of the Kent County Community Pasture. It is one of the many fascinating and funny tales which has been told in the Amos family for years. Although Mr. Amos is of English descent, the story bears traces of the Irish tradition.

There once was an old widow-woman who lived all by herself in the country. Her children were grown up and her husband had been dead for many years, so she had to look after herself and make her own way in the world. She kept a cow, some hens, a couple of pigs, raised her own vegetables and she was pretty independent. But, as often happens, trouble came to her.

Her cow took sick. She doctored the cow as best she could, but the cow did not get better. She called in the cow doctor and he did what he could to help the poor animal, but still, the beast did not improve. The old lady was in despair for she was afraid she was going to lose her cow and she did not know what to do.

Living in the area was a Bishop. He was a young man and he was very interested in the well-being of the people in his parish. He was always willing to help anybody with anything at anytime. Everyone knew how kind and obliging he was. So, the old woman went to the Bishop and asked him to come and see what he could do for her sick cow.

"Madame," said the Bishop, "I have no knowledge about cows, but I will go and see the animal if you think it will help you."

"Yes," said the widow, "I want you to come and see the cow. If the cow dies after you've seen it, I at least will be satisfied that I've done everything I can to save her."

So, the good Bishop went to visit the cow and the widow followed him out to the paddock where the cow was lying down. The Bishop put his hand on the cow's nose. He ran his hand over the back of its head. He pulled out its tongue and felt it. Then he walked around the cow and looked at it from the other side. He was puzzled. He didn't know anything at all about cows, but he did want to comfort the old lady. What on earth was he going to say? He walked around the animal three times, trying to think of something. Finally, in desperation, the Bishop shook his head and said,

"You poor beast. If you live, you live; if you die, you die, and nothing more can I do." And he went away.

Strangely enough, the cow got better. And the widow-woman was convinced that the Bishop had saved her cow.

Time passed, and a few years later the Bishop himself took sick. He had a terrible poisonous abscess on the inside of his throat and the swelling of it threatened to choke him to death. The doctor could not do anything for him and the Bishop's condition grew worse and worse.

When the old woman heard of the Bishop's trouble, she went to see him. She put her hand on his nose. She rubbed the back of his head. His tongue was already protruding from his mouth, so she felt it. Then she walked around the bed three times and stood and looked at him.

"You poor beast," she said. "If you live, you live; if you die, you die, and nothing more can I do."

The Bishop remembered that these were the very same words he had spoken to the woman's cow and he convulsed with laughter. He laughed so hard that the abscess inside his throat broke open, the poison drained out and the swelling went down.

Miraculously, the Bishop recovered and lived to carry on his good works in the parish for many years to come.

Do You Want To Buy A Cow?

This delightful tale was told by Madame Duguay of Lameque, New Brunswick. She told the story to Edith Butler, who recorded it for Ken Homer in the early 1960's. Ken Homer gave the tape to Professor Sandy Ives, who deposited it in the Northeast Archives of Folklore and Oral History at the University of Maine, which is where I found it in 1975.

Ti-Jean is a character common to Acadian folklore and although he is often portrayed as a numbskull, it becomes pretty clear at the end of these stories that Ti-Jean is not so dumb after all.

Once long ago there was a young man by the name of Ti-Jean who lived with his wife in a small cabin near the village of Lameque. Ti-Jean was very poor and all he owned was a cow. One morning, Ti-Jean woke up, stretched and yawned, and said to his wife.

"What's for breakfast, wife?"

"Nothing," replied the wife.

"Nothing? What do you mean . . . nothing? I am very hungry!"

"There is nothing to eat," answered the wife, "because the cupboard is bare and I have no money to buy food."

"Mon Doux!" said Ti-Jean. "We shall starve. Whatever shall I do?"

"You will have to sell the cow, dear husband. It is all we have left."

"Very well," said Ti-Jean. "It is a very sad thing to have to sell my beautiful cow, but t'would be sadder still to see us starve. I will go now and sell it."

He tied a piece of rope around the cow's neck and led him toward the village to see if he could find somebody who wanted to buy the cow. The first person he met coming down the road was the mayor.

"Good morning, Monsieur Mayor," said Ti-Jean.

"Good morning, Ti-Jean. How are you today?"

"Oh . . . I'm not so good," said Ti-Jean. "I am very sad because I have to sell my cow."

"Too bad!" said the mayor. "That is a very fine looking animal. But I can always use a new cow for myself. How much do you want for it?"

"I want fifty dollars," said Ti-Jean.

"Fifty dollars, eh? All right . . . it's a deal." The mayor reached into his pocket and he gave Ti-Jean his fifty dollars. Then he said,

"As you can see. I am on my way to an important meeting in the village and I can't take the cow with me. Would you be so kind as to put the cow in the pasture behind my house?"

"Yes, I will do that," said Ti-Jean.

"Thank-you," said the mayor, "and good-day."

Ti-Jean started off in the direction of the mayor's house, but before he got very far he met the parish priest.

"Good morning, Ti-Jean," said the priest.

"Good morning, father," said Ti-Jean.

"My, my, that is a lovely cow you have there. You are not going to sell it by any chance, are you?"

"Well, I was going to sell it . . ." said Ti-Jean.

"Good. Good! Splendid!! How much?"

"Fifty dollars."

"That's a fair price," said the priest. "I will give you fifty dollars." And he handed the money to Ti-Jean. "But, I have a little problem, and perhaps you would take care of it for me. I am going to church to say mass and I can't take the cow with me. Would you put it in my barn?"

"Very well," said Ti-Jean. "I will do that!"

"Thank-you," said the priest, "and good-day."

Again, Ti-Jean took the rope and began to lead the cow towards the priest's barn, but before he got there he met the doctor.

"Good morning, Monsieur Doctor," said Ti-Jean. "How do you like my cow? Would you like to buy it from me?"

"Oh, Ti-Jean," said the doctor, "it is a beautiful cow. Indeed, I would like to buy it. How much are you selling it for?"

"Fifty dollars," said Ti-Jean.

"Fifty dollars is a good price for a cow like that. But, I have to call on a patient who is very sick. Would you take the cow home for me?"

"Yes. I will do that gladly," said Ti-Jean as he pocketed the money.

"Thank-you," said the doctor, "and good-day."

So, Ti-Jean turned around and he took the cow home, for that was what the doctor had told him to do. Needless to say, he was feeling very pleased with himself for he had collected one hundred and fifty dollars and he still had his cow. When he arrived at the door of his little cabin, he called out to his wife,

"Come wife. Come see what your Ti-Jean has done. I have made one hundred and fifty dollars and I have brought back the cow."

But, when he told his wife of all that had happened that day, instead of being pleased and proud . . . she was very alarmed.

"Ti-Jean! Ti-Jean!" she scolded. "You have done a very stupid thing. You have cheated the mayor and the priest and the doctor, and that will land us in serious trouble."

"Mon Doux! Mon Doux!" cried Ti-Jean. "Whatever shall I do?"

"Go and fetch the lawyer," said the wife. "He will know how to get us out of this terrible mess."

The lawyer came. And when he was told of what had happened, he laughed and laughed. And then he stopped laughing and started to think. He thought very seriously, and he thought for a long time. Finally he stood up and said,

"I know what to do. I know how to defend you. I will argue that you are crazy and that you are not responsible for your actions. But, the mayor and the priest and the doctor must believe our story, so Ti-Jean, when you are asked for the money or the cow, you must reply by singing this silly song:

Tee dum tee dum tee diddle de dum
Tee dum tee diddle de dum
Tee dum tee dum tee diddle de dum
Tee dum tee diddle de dum.

"Very well," said Ti-Jean. "That sounds easy. I think I can do that."

Next day, there came an angry knock on the cabin door. It was the mayor.

"Good-day, Monsieur Mayor," said the lawyer. "Come in, we were expecting you."

"I have come to see that Ti-Jean goes to jail, for he has cheated me," said the mayor shaking his fists.

"Now, now. Don't be so harsh," argued the lawyer. "Poor Ti-Jean is sick in the head. He is crazy, and no-one can blame him for what he has done. You can't put him in jail if he is crazy, you know that, Mr. Mayor."

"Maybe so," replied the mayor. "But I will not be made a fool of. I must have my money or my cow!"

"Ask Ti-Jean and see for yourself," said the lawyer.

"Ti-Jean? Could I please have my cow or my fifty dollars?" begged the mayor.

"Ti-Jean smiled his most idiotic smile, and then he sang:

Tee dum tee dum tee diddle de dum
Tee dum tee diddle de dum
Tee dum tee dum tee diddle de dum
Tee dum tee diddle de dum.

"Oh! . . . . Goodness Gracious! . . . . You poor man!!" said the mayor, very much taken aback. "You are indeed crazy. Keep the money and the cow, it's the least I can do for someone as badly off as you." And the mayor went away with tears in his eyes for Ti-Jean's misfortune.

Soon there was another knock on the door. It was the priest.

"Ti-Jean," he scolded, "you have been very bad. You have cheated your priest. You must give me the cow or give back my fifty dollars."

"Father," said the lawyer, "Ti-Jean is not well. He is crazy and he knew not what he did when he sold you the cow and took your money. Have mercy on him."

The priest looked at Ti-Jean and Ti-Jean looked back at him with a mad and empty stare, and then he began to sing:

Tee dum tee dum tee diddle de dum
Tee dum tee diddle de dum
Tee dum tee dum tee diddle de dum
Tee dum tee diddle de dum.

"Oh, Ti-Jean," said the priest. "I can see that you are quite, quite mad. How very sad it is! Keep your money and your cow, and I will pray for you to get better."

After the priest left, the doctor arrived. He was furious, and like the rest, he demanded his money or the cow.

"You are a doctor," said the lawyer. "Can't you see that Ti-Jean is very ill? He is sick in the head and you must not demand anything from him, for that would make him worse."

The doctor went over to Ti-Jean to examine him, and Ti-Jean rolled his eyes and stuck out his tongue and then he burst into song:

Tee dum tee dum tee diddle de dum
Tee dum tee diddle de dum
Tee dum tee dum tee diddle de dum
Tee dum tee diddle de dum.

"Oh yes," said the doctor. "Yes, indeed. I can see that he is very sick. He is sick in the head. Ti-Jean, you must keep the money and the cow and don't you worry about a thing. You must have lots of rest and good care. Good luck and good-day."

When the door closed for the last time, they all burst out laughing and congratulated one another for fooling the mayor and the priest and the doctor . . and, on keeping both the cow and the one hundred and fifty dollars.

"Monsieur Lawyer, that was an excellent defence," joked the wife.

"Yes," said the lawyer. "It was. And now Ti-Jean, you must pay me. Ti-Jean shook his head.

"No." he said.

"No?" said the lawyer, very much surprised. "And why not?"

"Because," said Ti-Jean . . . . .

Tee dum tee dum tee diddle de dum
Tee dum tee diddle de dum
Tee dum tee dum tee diddle de dum
Tee dum tee diddle de dum.

Gabe Acquin and the Prince of Wales

*The story of Gabe Acquin is a legend which has a basis in fact. The early history books of New Brunswick invariably mention this remarkable man and anecdotes about his striking personality are not hard to find. There is no doubt that Gabe was a friend of Manners-Sutton and he did appear in London at Queen Victoria's Jubilee. The legend comes from old journals and history books, but Dr. Peter Paul from Carleton County told me part of the story and showed me a collection of **calling** cards and invitations received by Gabe from the British nobility. Whether Gabe actually did and said all the things attributed to him is open to conjecture. Nevertheless, these anecdotes are still part of an oral tradition.*

At St. Mary's on the Saint John River, the Indian people tell proud stories of their great Sagamore, Gabe Acquin. And even though he lived more than a hundred years ago, his people remember still how strong and handsome he was and that he was both resourceful and wise in his dealings with the white man.

Gabe knew more about the woods and the creatures who lived there than anyone else in the whole province of New Brunswick. He spoke the language of the musquash and the moose, of the mink and the beaver and the deer. He knew where every animal lived and even where the slippery, silent fish were hiding in the depths of the streams and brooks which flowed throughout the forests.

So great was his knowledge, that all the grandest gentlemen, the most prominent citizens, and the most important officers in the British army would travel for many miles to see Gabe and beg him to take them hunting or fishing. They themselves knew little about the mysteries of the forest, although they longed to go there to capture a big moose or a bear or to catch many fish. But, without an experienced man like Gabe to guide them, many had little hope of catching anything — except perhaps a cold or rheumatism or some other unpleasant thing.

It happened that a little way up the river from Gabe's house on the other side of the brilliant blue water of the Saint John, there was a huge mansion built of stone, surrounded by luxurious gardens and green lawns and large elm trees. In the mansion lived the Right Honourable J.H.T. Manners-Sutton. He was a very important person because he represented the Queen. He was so important that when people spoke to the Right Honourable J.H.T. Manners-Sutton, they began by saying "Your Excellency," or "Your Honour," — or something grand like that. But, when all was said and done, Manners-Sutton was the man's name, and "Sutton" is what Gabe called him.

Sutton and Gabe were good friends. Often they went hunting and fishing together and sometimes they would stay in the forest for many days. If Sutton wanted a bear, Gabe would set the trap — for nobody could set a trap like Gabe. If Sutton wanted a moose, Gabe would strip some bark off a tree and call the moose to him — for nobody could call a moose like Gabe. And, if Sutton wanted to eat, Gabe would cook him a fine meal — for nobody could cook quite like Gabe. In fact, there wasn't much that Gabe didn't do for Sutton when they were in the woods, and, in return, there wasn't much that Sutton wouldn't do for Gabe if he could. Sometimes though, Gabe's requests were very difficult to grant. And when Sutton had to refuse, Gabe used all his resourcefulness and wisdom to persuade the Governor to do as he wanted.

One day when they were out fishing by the side of a deep stream and catching many fish, Gabe said to his friend,

"Sutton, you are a very important man. You represent the Queen. I want you to do something for me and my people."

"What is it you want, Gabe?"

"I want you to change the law. Me and my people get very thirsty and we would like to buy rum and whiskey and ale to quench our thirst, but the law of the land forbids it."

Now, the truth of the matter was that Sutton liked nothing better than rum and whiskey and ale himself, and he disliked the law every bit as much as Gabe did. But all the same, his answer was no.

"I would like to help you my friend," said Sutton, "but I can't change the law of the land without dismissing our present government. I would have to bring in new lawmakers and that is very expensive and almost impossible for me to do."

But Gabe wouldn't take no for an answer and he kept pestering the Governor until he drove him almost crazy. Still, Sutton said no.

So, one night when Sutton was fast asleep in their little cabin in the woods, Gabe crept out of bed and went outside into the night, bolting the door behind him. He crouched in the darkness and waited. Whether Gabe did it deliberately or not, we'll never know, but suddenly the little cabin caught fire and the Governor could not get out.

"Help! Help!!" he cried as he banged against the bolted door. "Get me out of here! Let me out!!"

"Sutton," shouted Gabe through the loud crackling of the flames, "I will not let you out until you promise to do as I ask. You must change the law of the land so that my people can quench their thirst.''

"Yes! Yes!!'' wailed Sutton. "I'll do anything you want. I promise. Now, for pity's sake, open the door!''

Gabe opened the door, and a very indignant Lieutenant Governor staggered out. He was covered from head to toe in black soot. They spoke not a word to each other, but packed up what remained of their gear and went home. And when they got to Fredericton, Sutton went to the parliament building and dismissed the old government and brought in new law-makers. The first thing the new law-makers did was to change the law of the land so that Gabe and his people and everyone else could buy rum and whiskey and ale to quench their thirst.

"Ah,'' said Gabe. "My friend Sutton is a man of honour. He keeps his word. I will take him hunting and fishing again.''

So it came to pass that Gabe and the Governor went hunting and fishing again. And after Sutton had caught all he wanted of deer and bear and mink, Gabe said to him,

"Sutton, you are a very important man. You represent the Queen. I wish you to grant me another favour.''

"Well,'' said Sutton, "what is it this time? I will not change the law of the land again.''

"No,'' said Gabe. "I would not ask you to change the law of the land again. Once is enough. But, I know that you have big parties in your stone house and you invite the officers of the British Regiment, you invite the wealthy citizens, you invite the members of Government and sometimes you invite me, but never have you invited my people of St. Mary's. I want you to invite my people to your house of stone.''

"But Gabe,'' protested the Governor, "your people would not enjoy the customs of my house. My ways are not your ways and they would not be happy there.''

"No,'' said Gabe. "My people will be happy. Perhaps it is your friends who would not be happy. Please do as I wish.''

"Very well,'' said the Governor. "I'll see what I can do.''

At Christmas time, Sutton threw a big party, and true to his word, he invited Gabe and the Indian people from St. Mary's. It was a grand occasion. The Governor's people wore their very best holiday finery — the men in elegant suits and tall hats, the ladies in long evening dresses. The Indians of St. Mary's had soft caribou coats while the women wore beaded dresses which came down to their ankles.

The string band began to play waltzes and quadrilles and when the Governor's friends were through dancing around the ballroom, Gabe and his people nodded their approval. Then the Indian women brought forth a large drum and began to beat out strange haunting rhythms which throbbed and echoed throughout the stillness of the room. The men lined up one behind the other and tramped up and down the ballroom making lively gestures with their arms and legs, and throwing back their heads, they chanted loudly to the thump, thump, thump of the drums. The audience was spellbound and when the dancing had ended they clapped heartily. Much to the Governor's surprise, the party was a marvellous success, and Sutton was so pleased that he invited Gabe and his people to his house every Christmas for years and years after that.

One summer, when Gabe and the Governor had returned from a long sojourn in the forest, Gabe said,

"Sutton, you are a very important person. You represent the Queen. I want you to do something for me. I am told that soon you will have a visitor."

"Yes," said Sutton. "The Prince himself is coming from England to stay with me. In fact, he is coming tomorrow."

"I want to meet him," said Gabe. "I have never seen a Prince before."

"No," said Sutton. "The Prince will be very busy. He will not have time to meet you."

And no matter how much Gabe tried to persuade him, the Governor would not give in.

Next day, Gabe climbed into his canoe and paddled up the river until he came to the back of the Governor's house. He waited there a long time, and when nothing happened he came home. He did the same thing day after day until finally, one morning, Gabe saw the figure of a strange solitary man walking in the garden at the back of the house. The stranger began to walk down to the river to get a better look at the dusky-skinned man who was sitting in the middle of the river in his funny little boat. Gabe, in turn, paddled closer to shore to see if he could find out who the pale-faced stranger might be. As Gabe drew near, the stranger beckoned and called out:

"You there. Come over here."

Gabe paddled ashore, and when he came right up to the man, he was certain it was the Prince himself.

"Who are you anyway?" asked the Prince. "And what kind of boat is that?"

"I'm Gabe . . . and this here is a canoe. It is made from the bark of a birch tree. Get in, Prince. I will show you how to paddle."

"Yes indeed," replied the Prince. "That is precisely what I intended to do."

But, as soon as they started to move out into the river, a great mob of people ran forth from the Governor's house. They yelled and shouted and waved their arms frantically in the air.

"Come back!" they screamed. "Come back . . . come back!!"

But, the Prince turned to Gabe and told him to row as fast as he could. Gabe paddled down the Saint John River and he paddled up the Nashwaak River and he paddled all morning until the Prince became very hungry and wanted to go home for lunch. On the way back, Gabe told the Prince all about himself and his people at St. Mary's and the Prince told Gabe what it was like to be the son of a Queen and to live in England.

"You must come to my country and visit me. I will send a big ship to carry you across the wide ocean to England. Please bring your birch bark boat with you to show to my people."

It was some time after that when Gabe left from Halifax on a big steamer. When he got to England, he stayed in a place called Kensington Gardens and in the middle of the gardens was a lake in which Gabe paddled his canoe. There was a Great Celebration going on in England at that time, and people came from all over the world to see Gabe and his birch back canoe. Most of them had never seen a Canadian Indian before and when they saw Gabe they were very much impressed.

Of course, everybody wanted a ride in the canoe, including the Princes and the Princesses and the Lords and the Dukes and the Earls. In fact, all the Royal Family went with Gabe in his canoe, except for the Queen. The Queen's name was Victoria. She was old and fat and very cranky, and when the Prince tried to tell her what fun it was to paddle in a canoe, she made a sour face and replied,

"We are not amused."

And that was that.

But Gabe didn't mind, because the Lords and the Dukes and the Earls wrote him wonderful letters full of praise and they thanked him for the canoe ride and they asked him to dinner. Gabe got to visit some of the very best palaces and large estates in England and he was given gold and silver and valuable jewels as presents to take home with him.

By the time that Gabe got back to St. Mary's, he must have been as rich as any Lord, and it's a wonder he didn't build himself a great mansion of stone right next to Sutton's place — as proof of his social success. But, that wasn't Gabe's way of doing things. Instead, he lived quietly in his modest house for a long time after that, and he hunted and fished with his friends until he died a very old and happy man, much honoured and respected by all who knew him.

Although these things happened many years ago, the mansion of stone where Sutton lived and where Gabe met the Prince can still be seen in the city of Fredericton. And right to this very day, Gabe's people live at the St. Mary's Reserve on the other side of the sparkling blue waters of the St. John River. As for myself, I have seen the book wherein Gabe pasted the letters and invitations from the Lords and the Dukes and the Earls of England — and I guess that at least part of the story must be true.

The Man Who Plucked the Gorbey

The Man Who Plucked the Gorbey is a story which was told in the lumber camps of New Brunswick and Maine. Anyone who tells the tale will always swear that it really happened and will tell you the name of the man who did the deed. I guess there must be a dozen or more men who are supposed to have plucked the Gorbey at one time or another, and there is a story in England about a sparrow who lost his feathers in a similar way. But, the Gorbey story has become so thoroughly adapted to the Maritimes that it seems to be "one of our own". Stories about the Canada Jay are legion and I've collected several anecdotes about the bird which are included with the main tale. I collected these anecdotes and stories in 1975-76 from several different people: Frank Munn of Storeytown, Wilmot MacDonald of Glenwood, Clarence Curtis of Newcastle, Irvine Van Horne of Bloomfield Ridge, and Tom Francoeur of Lorne Settlement, to name a few.

Ordinary birds, like ordinary people, sometimes behave in a very strange and un-ordinary way.

Take Old Ferguson, for instance. I don't suppose you ever heard tell of that notorious old bird, because he lived a very long time ago. He was a Canada Jay, and the lumbermen in the woods in back of Boiestown named him after a friend of theirs who drowned one spring as the result of drunken driving. The poor fellow slipped from the log he was riding down the mighty Miramichi, and some would tell you that the spirit of that man actually lived on within the breast of the rascally grey bird. Maybe it was so, because the man Ferguson was known as an awful greedy-guts before he died, and the bird was a regular old gorbey, just like him. For another thing, the man and the bird sort of looked alike: both wore grey coats and a black hat.

It happened that whenever the men sat down to eat their mid-day meal at the lunch-hole, Old Ferguson and his gang of feathered friends waited silently in the trees. They watched while the wood was gathered, and while the fire was made, and while the snow melted slowly in the kettle for tea. But as soon as the lids on the lunch pails popped open, out they came in sudden, swirling, streaks of grey.

Old Ferguson would be the first to take aim at a woodsman. Then he swooped down. And as soon as the man was ready to bite into his biscuit, the bird snatched it from his hand. The rest of the jays were almost as brave, and just as clever at getting food. After they were fed, one or two played hide-and-seek by disappearing under a coat-tail, up a sleeve or pant-leg, or even on top of his head where the woodsman couldn't see him at all. The men laughed. They were happy to share their food and they called the birds greedy Gorbies because they ate so much. But, as usual, Old Ferguson ate more than everybody else. So, they thought they would teach him a lesson.

One afternoon, the sawyer poured his whiskey into a mug, soaked some biscuits in it and spread the feast out on the end of a log.

"There ya go," he called. And the Gorbies swarmed around and ate every bit. Of course, Old Ferguson wasn't satisfied. He begged for more, and more. And the more he ate of the delicious whiskey-soaked biscuit, the more excited and confused he became.

"Whooppee!" he shouted, as he zig-zagged and zoomed upwards, landing very unsteadily in the crotch of a tree. "Whee!"

Soon, it started to get dark, and all the more sensible birds flew away. They were scared of being caught by the hawks and owls that came out to hunt smaller birds at night. But Old Ferguson just puffed out his feathers and swaggered and swore that he didn't care for the biggest owl or meanest hawk that was in the forest, he was going to stay. And he did. And he got so drunk that he couldn't tell left from right, or in from out, or up from down, and he flew right into a tree, and knocked himself out.

A lumberman picked him up, dumped him into a warm mitt, and carried him back to camp. He rubbed the scrawny legs and soft wings to see if the bird was hurt. It lay quite still for a while, but then the dark eyes blinked, the wings stuttered and stirred, and Old Ferguson wobbled onto his feet.

"Well, I reckon you're well enough now," said the woodsman. "But before I let you go, mind me well, and don't take more than a bird's share of whiskey again!" Then he stripped the waxed string from a piece of baloney and tied it round the bird's neck in a bow. And for many seasons after that, whenever the men returned to camp, they would be greeted by Old Ferguson wearing his baloney bow and shouting,

"Whee! Whee! Whooppee!"

Some people call the Canada Jay a Whiskey-jack, and you can see why. The Indian name for the bird sounds like Whiskey-jack too, but the Indians called him that for quite a different reason. Wisk-i-djak was their word for the mighty spirit that lived inside the bird. And whenever they went to hunt for moose, they stopped and listened for the voice of the Spirit-bird to guide them through the woods to where the large animal was.

Wisk-i-djak liked moose-meat just as much as he liked whiskey. But when the lumbermen weren't around, he would have to get by on a poor meal of fleas and ticks picked from the moose's back. Sometimes, a hunter came through the woods, and then the bird screeched and hollared to get his attention.

Crack! went the sound of a rifle, and the moose staggered and toppled over in a heap of fur and antlers. Then the bird fluttered from out of the branches and settled triumphantly on the horns of his dead friend.

"Gee! Gee!" he exclaimed. "Hungree!" Finally, the man gave Wisk-i-djak his reward, and the bird flew away with its belly full. If the Canada Jay could pull a clever trick like that, it's no wonder people told stories about him and that they thought he was haunted.

Another story that every woodsman knows concerns a certain man who came to work in a lumber camp during an exceptionally cold winter. He was terribly ugly and bad-tempered, but he had a wonderful crop of curly, black hair of which he was extremely proud. The man didn't like Gorbies. When the birds flew near him at the lunch-hole, he swatted them with his hand, and he cursed at them when they stole his food. At last one day, when he was particularly hungry, one of the birds snatched his food and the man flew into an horrendous rage. The crew scrambled to their feet to see what was wrong.

"It's that blasted Camp Robber stealing my food again," he bellowed. " — And I'm gonna learn that bird a lesson when I get my hands on him!"

"I wouldn't harm one of them birds if I was you," said one of the men.

"Yaas," agreed the other. "It's bad luck to harm a Gorbey. Awful bad luck,"

"Thats the biggest bunch of lies I ever heard," said the man. "And any feller who believes in that is a darn fool . . what's more, I'll prove it!"

He held out more food for the Gorbey to take, and when the bird landed, the man lurched forward and grabbed it in both hands. He took the bird and plucked every feather from its back and chest until the poor creature was almost naked. Then, the Gorbey flew up into the air with a mighty squawk and dropped dead at the man's feet.

The lumbermen shook their heads. "You'll be sorry for that," they said. "Something will happen now, for sure."

The man just smiled to himself. "Nothing could happen to me because of a silly bird," he thought.

Little did he know what morning would bring. For when he awoke and looked in the mirror and went to comb his wonderful crop of curly, black hair . . . it all fell out! His head was as bare as a peeled log. And from that day to this, not even so much as a whisker grew back in.

Nobody knows for sure what happened that day, but many believe that the Gorbey's spirit came back and had its revenge. And nobody knows for sure who the man was. But, if ever you see an old lumberman whose head is as bare as a peeled log, you might ask him . . .

"Are you the man who plucked the Gorbey?"

Three Gold Hairs From the Giant's Back

Wilmot MacDonald of Glenwood told me this story in the summer of 1975. He's told it lots of times to lots of people, but the place where it was told the most was in the lumber camps along the Portage River. Between supper time and lights out, Wilmot and his friend Clarence Curtis entertained themselves and their friends by telling marvelous tales about ghosts and giants and other magical beings.

This story has been found in the Acadian culture and it also appears in Grimm's Fairy Tales. With all due respect to the Brothers Grimm, I like the way Wilmot tells it best, perhaps because Wilmot's version has a Maritime flavour.

I'm gonna tell you a story about an old fella who had four or five sons. And he had one son who he thought was kind of stupid. But anyway, an old king was walking by their door one Sunday afternoon and he said,

"You've got a fine crowd of boys there, old man."

"Yes, I have," said the old man. "And that fella over there is gonna marry your daughter."

"What? Marry my daughter?" said the king.

"Sure," said the old fella. "He's gonna marry your daughter, and he's leavin' for the castle this afternoon. I want you to write him a note telling him where to go and who to see when he gets there."

The king wasn't too happy about that because the old man's son wasn't a fine prince and didn't have very much money either.

"A-ha!," thought the king. "I guess I'll have him killed. That'll fix him!" He took some paper and an envelope out of his pocket and wrote on it:

BEHEAD THIS MAN JUST AS SOON AS HE GETS TO MY CASTLE

He showed the letter to the young fella, but the son couldn't read it. Then, he folded the paper, sealed it in an envelope and gave it to the boy.

"When you get to my place, give this letter to the queen. She will look after you."

"Thank you," said the young fella. And away he went.

The young man travelled all afternoon and when it got dark, he walked up an old woods road. There was a fire burning, just a small fire. So he went up and there he found a tramp. An old bum. He was sittin' down having something to eat and warming himself in front of the campfire.

"Have something to eat," said the tramp. He had lots of grub with him. So, the young fella and the old tramp had a big feed.

"Where are you going anyway?" said the tramp.

"I am going to the king's castle to marry the king's daughter."

The old tramp had more sense than the young fella did and he said, "Whoever told you to do that? Do you really expect her to marry the likes of you?"

"Oh, yes. I have a note from the king right here in my pocket."

The tramp didn't say anything, but waited until the young fella went to sleep. Then, he went through his pockets, found this letter, and he opened it, and he read it. When he saw what the king had written, he tore the letter up and wrote another letter in the king's handwriting which said:

THIS YOUNG MAN MUST MARRY MY DAUGHTER AS SOON AS HE ARRIVES

The tramp sealed the letter in an envelope and put it back into the boy's pocket.

The next morning when the young fella woke up, he bid the tramp good morning and he struck out. When he landed at the old king's place they didn't know him from Tom the Devil. So, he gave the Queen his note. She showed it to her daughter.

"Daughter, this letter is from the king. He says you are to marry this young man right away. So, hurry up. Get going. I want it done before your father gets home."

Pretty soon, the king came home.

"What did you do with that young fella who wanted to marry our daughter?"

"Well dear," said the queen, "they're away getting married."

"Married! I didn't put that on the letter! You were supposed to kill him. Didn't you read it?"

"Oh, yes. I read it. That's what's on the letter and it's in your handwriting."

"Where is it? Let me see it!!" He looked and he saw that it was his writing and he was real mad.

"He may have married her, but I'll make sure that he never gets to live with her. Ha! I know just what to do with him."

Soon, the young man and the princess came home to the castle. The old king was sittin' there waiting for them.

"Look-it! Before you can live with that woman, you've got to go to the giant and get the three gold hairs from out of that giant's back and bring them to me. Then, and only then, can you live with my daughter as your wife."

So, away he started. It was a long journey, and he stopped off at a farmer's house to have some dinner. He told the farmer that he was going to see the giant and that he had to get the three gold hairs for the king.

"I'm gonna tell you somethin'," said the farmer. "If you ever get talking to that giant, — and I don't expect you will — but if you do, ask him a question for me. Ask him how it is that I've got one tree in my orchard grows one kind of fruit on one side and another kind of fruit on the other side."

The young fella said he would and he continued on his way.

He travelled until night time. Then, he was invited into a man's house to have his supper. He told the man where he was going and what he had to do.

"You're crazy boy, to do a thing like that. He'll kill you just as soon as you get there."

"Well, I got a woman, and I can't live with her, so I might as well be dead anyway," said the young fella.

"Nobody has ever gone to that giant's house and come out of there alive. But, if you ever get talking to that giant, would you ask him something for me? Ask him how come my wife, who was once so kind and pretty, is now so mean and hateful I can hardly stand to live with her."

"Yes, I will," said the young man. And he went away.

Soon, he came to a river. There was no bridge and there was no boat, so he sat down on the river bank and thought, "How am I gonna get across this river to the giant's house on the other side?"

By and by, a great ghost appeared on the scene. He came swimming out of the water and he sat down and he talked to him. "Well," he said, "come on."

"You mean I have to cross the river on your back?"

"Yes. 'fraid so. I'm the only kind of ferry boat there is around here, so you'd better get on if you want to get to the other side."

The boy hopped onto the ghost's back and they swam across. When they got there, the ghost asked him where he was going. He told him.

"That giant's a pretty scary fella," said the ghost. "But you might be lucky and get what you want. So, if you ever get talking to him, will you ask how come I have to ferry so many people across this river. I never get any money or thanks for it."

"Yes, I will," said the young man.

Finally, he arrived at the giant's door and the giant's wife let him in. He explained why he had come and he told her the three questions he had promised to ask.

"You'll have to be very careful and very quiet," said the giant's wife. "My husband eats men like you. But, you go in and curl up underneath the bed and stay there. I'll do the best I can to help you."

No sooner had he crawled under the giant's bed when the giant himself came home.

"Fee, Fi, Fo, Fum. I smell the blood of an Englishman!"

"No, you don't. You don't smell the likes of that a'tall," said his wife. "It's just the meat cooking on the stove for dinner."

"Oh. Well, maybe so," said the giant.

She put the supper on the table and the giant sat down and he went to work and he ate it. He ate the whole side of a cow, a bag of potatoes, nineteen cups of tea, two loaves of bread, and then he rolled into bed. His wife did up the supper dishes and then crawled into bed with him to see what she could do. When the giant was snoring away, she reached over and jerked one of the hairs from his back and dropped it down behind the bed. The young man caught it and dropped the hair in his little chocolate box.

The giant woke up. "What's the matter with you tonight?" he growled.

"Oh giant," she said, "I can't sleep. I dreamed of a man who had a fruit tree which grew one kind of fruit on one side and another kind of fruit on the other side."

"Well," he said, "If that damn fool would dig up the pot of gold that's under his tree, he'd have fruit that grew the same and he'd have enough money to do him the rest of his life."

After a while, the giant went back to sleep. The wife reached over and pulled out another gold hair. This time it hurt pretty bad.

"Ouch!" roared the giant. "What's going on here?"

"Oh giant," replied the wife, "don't be angry. I was dreaming about a fella who married a lovely girl. She was so nice looking and now she's grown so homely and hateful, he can't stand to live with her."

"If that damn fool wasn't so mean and stingy, his wife would be pretty enough," replied the giant.

The wife waited until the giant was sound asleep, then she pulled out the third gold hair. This time, the giant jumped up and kicked her in the side, he was so angry.

"Oh giant, don't kill me. I can't sleep. I'm twisting and turning and dreaming about a ghost who ferries men across the river and gets no money or thanks for it."

"He's another damn fool, " said the giant. "The next time he swims a man across the river, he should heave him off and let him drown and let that man's ghost ferry in his place."

Now that the young man had his three gold hairs and the answer to his three questions, he waited until both the giant and his wife went back to sleep. And then . . . Mr. Man! he just hot-footed it right out that door and down to that river!!

"Tell me," said the ghost. "Were you talking to the giant?"

"Yup. I was talking to him"

"What did he say about me?"

"Let me sit down for a minute and think about it. I was so scared I thought he would kill me a dozen times!"

"Well, get on my back anyway, and come on over."

When they got to the other side, the young man said, "Look-it. That giant told me to tell you that the next time you catch a man going to his house and botherin' him, you head him off, and throw him in the river and drown him and let his ghost ferry in your place."

"Good bye!" said the ghost. "That's just what I'll do."

Then the young man went to see the fellow with the ugly wife. They was up and havin' breakfast.

"What did the giant say about me wife?" he asked.

"Well, now, I don't like to tell you."

"Oh, yes," he said, "Tell me!"

"He told me that if you weren't so mean and stingy, your wife would be pretty enough."

The wife thought that was a very good answer. She stopped firing bread pans and throwing flour around the house and within ten minutes she got so pretty he couldn't even look at her! The young man started on his way.

Soon, he reached the house of the farmer who owned the fruit tree. The man asked him,

"What did the giant say about the tree?"

I'll tell you what he said about that tree if you want to know. He said for you and me to go out and dig up the pot of gold under the fruit tree and to divide the money between us. Then the tree will grow fruit alike and you'll have enough money to last for the rest of your life."

So, they went with an axe and a pick and they dug up a big iron pot full of gold. It filled a bag for each of them and the man was so grateful, he gave the young fella his horse and his express wagon to go home.

"Never mind bringing it back," he said. "I have so much money, I don't care."

The young man took the horse and the express wagon and the bag of gold and the three gold hairs and he landed at the king's castle. Boys, I tell ya, he's a big man now!!

"Where'd you get all that?" said the king.

"Oh, I got it from the giant."

"What kind of person is that giant anyway?"

"He's just the nicest man you ever met! He gave me the bag of gold, he gave me the three gold hairs out of his back and he gave me a horse and an express wagon to bring it home in. Talk about a nice giant! That's the lovliest man in the world!"

So, the king said, "Give me that horse and that wagon and let me go!"

"Sure," said the young man. "I'll drive you there, if you don't know where to go."

He hitched up the horse to the wagon and the old king got on and they drove all the way to the river. The young fella helped the king down and led him to the river's edge.

"You'll have to cross the river on the ghost's back."

"Hop on," said the ghost.

The king hopped on the ghost's back. When they got half way across, the ghost threw the king off his back and drowned him and left the king's ghost to ferry in his place.

The young fella went back to the castle and took his woman away. They used the gold to build a place of their own. And, they lived happily ever after.

The Legend of Old Shan

Bayard Hoyt owns a tree-farming and lumbering operation in Sunbury County. He also keeps a small private museum of antique furniture, guns, peaveys, and farming implements, and has a huge collection of china and wooden horses. Besides all that, he's a great story-teller. Although Ogden Settlement has long been abandoned and only traces remain of the habitations around Wells's Corner, the legend of Old Shan is still very much alive, and over the years, the name "Old Shan" has become attached not only to the bear, but also to the trap that caught him.

In New Brunswick there is a place called Hoyt, and in Hoyt there is a man called Bayard and at Bayard's camp there is a big, rusty, bear-trap. In the jaws of the bear-trap lies a piece of brittle old bone.

"That trap is called Old Shan," declared Bayard. "I could tell you quite a story about that bear-trap if you'd care to listen . . ." And this is what he said:

"It was back in 1960, and I was lumbering out at Rocky Lake, way out back of Wirral. I had a man by the name of Joe Boucher working for me. He was a foreman and a scaler and a real fine fella. I thought a lot of him . . . and I do yet. Well anyway, he came into the camp one night lugging this great big heavy bear-trap on his shoulder. And when he got himself inside the door, he dropped the contraption on the floor.

"Joe, where'd you get that?" I said.

"Oh . . . way up there on top of the mountain somewheres. I didn't find the bear though. Maybe I'll go back tomorrow."

I looked at the trap, and it fascinated me. I could see that it was very old and that it was completely hand-made from start to finish. To my mind, it was a real work of art . . . the way it was bevelled and put together and everything, and I said,

"Joe, what are you going to do with this trap?"

"Oh," he says, "nothin'."

"Well look here, I'd like to have this trap for the camp."

"Sure," he said.

"But I wonder where it came from, exactly?"

"Well," said Joe, "I'll show you tomorrow."

But, the next day it snowed. Joe's tracks were covered up and we were never able to find the spot again. We never knew exactly where the trap came from. So anyway, I took the trap and hung it up on the outside of my camp. A few months later, a fella came by and looked at it for a long time, and finally he said,

"Where'd you get that?"

I said, "We found it out back of Rocky Lake ... up on the mountain."

He looked at it very carefully.

"Do you know it?" I said.

"I dunno," he replied, scratching his head. "I'm not sure ... but, it might be Old Shan."

"What's Old Shan?" I asked.

"Well," he said, "when I was a boy, back around the turn of the century, there was a trap around this country that became very, very famous. It was called Old Shan. And it disappeared. We hunted for it at South Branch, and Rocky Lake, and Oromocto Lake, and all over the place. And right to this day when we're out hunting, we look as much for that trap as we do for game. Nobody ever found it."

"Are you sure that's it?" I asked.

"No, I'm not. I wouldn't know it at all. But you ask Johnnie McAleer, and he'll know whether that's Old Shan or not."

"What's so famous about that trap anyway?" I asked. So, he told me.

"It seems that a long time ago, almost eighty years or so, there was a man came to live at Ogden Settlement. Ogden Settlement doesn't exist any more. The buildings have fallen down, and it's all grown up with trees, and there's not even a road in there. But, this man's name was George Wells, and he was a music teacher from Boston. He came up to New Brunswick to hunt, and he liked the country so well that he kept coming back. Finally, he decided to settle down. He couldn't make much money as a music teacher, so he learned to be a blacksmith instead. When he settled in, they called his place "Wells's Corner," after him and his shop. Now that's a fact. I know right well, because I've been to the spot a hundred times myself.

George Wells was a real artist. Anything he did, he did extremely well — whether it was music teaching, or building bob-sleds, or shoeing horses, or making bear-traps. He built a lot of bear-traps. But, he built one bear-trap that was better than all the rest. It became very, very famous because no matter where a man set that trap, he caught his bear. And there was never a bear got out of it. Many bears will cut their paws, or they'll bust the trap, or they'll do something ... but, whenever that trap was set, a bear was caught.

About that time, there came to the South Branch settlement the biggest, baddest, boldest bear that ever was seen. He killed the sheep in the fields, he killed the small animals in the yard, and, as if that weren't enough, he'd go to the well or spring where the farmers kept their milk and cream and he'd drink the milk and cream and smash the creamers up. He got so bad, he'd come right up to the barn door, tear the barn door off, and go in and kill a calf.

Well sir, back in those days people couldn't live with a menace like that around. They had to do something or the bear would clean them right out. So they did just about everything in the world they could think of to try to catch this bear. But, he was too smart for them.

First of all, they rigged up a string and attached one end to the barn door and the other end to the trigger of a gun which was lodged to a tree. And when the bear pawed at the barn door and moved the string, the bullet was supposed to fire off and hit him. But, somehow or another the bear always managed to work around it, for a bullet never so much as tickled a hair on his hide.

Then, the farmers began to stay up late at night to shoot at the bear when he went mauling around in the dark. But it seemed that whenever they took aim and fired . . . nothing would hit him, and he got away.

After that, the word went out all round the county, and all the best trappers came and set all kinds of different traps. But, they never could catch him.

The bear escaped certain death so often, people began to think he must be haunted. And everyone knew that the only way to catch a haunted bear was with silver bullets. The people in that little settlement didn't have much, but they gave everything they owned that was made of silver. Silver watches, silver spoons, coins, bracelets, and medallions, all went into a big iron pot to be melted down to make silver bullets. Then, the men took their muzzle-loaders and went out and shot at the haunted bear until every last bit of ammunition was used up. But, the bear escaped unharmed.

Needless to say, things got pretty desperate. They had to catch that bear or he was going to ruin them. Well then finally, someone remembered about Old Shan. Johnnie McAleer owned the trap that had been built by George Wells and McAleer lived over in the next settlement, so they went over there and asked him to use Old Shan to trap the bear. It was their last and only hope.

"Yes," said Johnnie, "I'll do it, and I think I can catch him. But, I've got to do it my own way."

"Well," they said, "we don't care how you do it . . . just so long as you get him."

Johnnie McAleer was a good woodsman. He knew that he wouldn't catch the bear at the barn, because the bear was too suspicious and wise. So, Johnnie just waited for a week or two and watched to see where the bear was coming from and where it lived. Then, he set his trap in the woods.

After a few days, he went back to the woods to tend his trap. And young Johnnie . . that's his boy . . went with him. When they got there, there was no trap. Old Shan was gone. The bushes were all ripped up, the trees were all broken down, and there was a patch through the woods like you would make with a bull-dozer today. They followed that path through the woods for miles and miles where the bear had slashed and had broken up everything that was in his way, trying to get rid of that trap. But, nobody ever heard tell of that bear again, and they never heard tell of the trap either. It was a mystery, and everybody wondered what had happened.''

Well, after I heard about the trap belonging to Johnnie McAleer, I went over to his place and I said,

''Johnnie, I think I've got a trap over at the camp that might belong to you.''

''No, you don't,'' he said. ''You've got no trap of mine, for I haven't set a trap for ten years.''

''What about Old Shan,'' I said. ''Do you know anything about that?''

''Old Shan!! Well . . . . that depends. What kind of shape was the trap in?''

''Very good shape,'' I said. ''But the springs are rusted and the pan is gone.'' The pan is a broad, flat-shaped thing like a tongue, and when the bear steps on that, the springs fly loose and the jaws clamp down and grab his paw.

So, Johnnie said, ''Just a minute.''

He disappeared and went down to his shed, and he was gone quite a little while. When he came back, he brought a pan for the bear-trap, and he said,

''I always kept this pan. I was with my father when he went out to tend Old Shan. Everything was broken down and the trap was gone . . . but we found the pan where the bear had ripped it off. We brought the pan home and I always kept it. Here . . . you take the pan. And if it fits the trap, you'll know that you found Old Shan.''

Now, I have the trap and I have the pan. They fit together perfectly. And that piece of bone you see gripped in the jaws of the rusty old trap is probably all that remains of the big, bad, bear. I don't think he ever got clear of the trap. I guess you could say that the mighty battle between Old Shan and the bear was a war that neither won, for they both lay locked-together up there on that mountain top for nearly eighty years, before Joe Boucher found them and I brought them back here. And that's them . . . hanging from the side of my camp.

The Old Pine Tree

About one hundred yards beyond Bayard Hoyt's house there is an ancient Baptist graveyard. Some of the stones are still standing but one grave is marked only by a huge pine tree. I asked why the grave was so special and Mr. Hoyt told me this story.

This is a very old story about a pine tree and it was told to me by my neighbour Miles Webb who was born around 1852. He's been dead a great many years now, but Miles told me how, as a young boy, he stood at the graveside when that tree was planted. I'm telling this story to you, not to prove anything, but because the story is a wonderful compliment to the old couple the pine tree represents.

There was a married couple by the name of Hughes who lived over on the Broad Road which is where Camp Gagetown is now. He was a Methodist and she was a Baptist, but they got along very well. They were a happy, contented couple and they never let religion interfere with their domestic life and happiness in any way. I've heard people say that there was never a quarrel in that house, and I think that's a marvelous thing. Even when they became very old, she went to her church and he went to his, and just before the old lady died, she asked her husband to bury her in the Baptist graveyard which is right here in my back yard. He was perfectly willing to carry out her wishes because they'd always lived that way and he figured that was how they should die.

After the service, the funeral procession travelled over this road and up Parson's Hill where the pine trees grew so thick their branches hung down over the road. The old gentleman was sitting on top of a horse-drawn carriage and he reached up and broke a twig off one of the trees. He carried it in his hand to the graveside.

When the burial was over, he went and he stuck the twig into the head of the grave. He said, "If it's better for Ma, this will live. If it's not better for Ma, It'll die."

Well now. There's been lots of twigs broken off lots of trees and stuck in the ground in lots of places, but never will one take root. I know, I've tried. But, he stuck it in the ground with those words; "If it's better for Ma, this will live. If it's not better for Ma, it'll die." Thats the story, and there's your tree right out there. And it's about the biggest tree in the forest around here.

The Maiden's Sacrifice

*This version of a Malecite legend is adapted from a poem in Ballads of
Acadia by the New Brunswick historian, James Hannay. Hannay calls the
Saint John River the "Wigoudi", which in Malecite means "an enclosed
place full of people". In fact "Wigoudi" was the Indian name for a
settlement or town on Navy Island at the upper end of Saint John harbour,
and the Malecite name for the Saint John River is "Wullustock".*

*Some people doubt that there ever was a princess called Malabeam,
and in an earlier version of the story collected by Silas T. Rand, this
romantic figure is not mentioned at all. Rand's story relates that the wives
of two Indian braves were taken captive by the Mohawk and were forced
to lead the war-party downstream to the Malecite village. Before the
Mohawk tumbled to their doom, the two women managed to escape and
lived to tell the tale. The interesting thing is that similar legends have
been told about Niagara Falls and about Iroquois Falls on the Abitibi
River. And a legend very much like Hannay's, complete with a princess,
has been recorded about the Kakabeka Falls on the Kaministiquia River
in North Western Ontario.*

Every day, Malabeam and her father Sacotis paddled their canoe up
the blue Wigoudi river and loaded their boat with salmon which swam in
the deep waters. And when they caught enough to feed themselves and
their family, Malabeam and Sacotis rested on the green banks of the river.
They liked the rays of the sun warming their skin and the soothing odour
of sweet grass in the summer air. Always, at night, they would return to
the quiet Malecite village which was their home.

The village was perched high on a bank above the swift and raging
torrent of Grand Falls. The people lived in peace, for their enemy the
Mohawk had departed long ago. The hatchet of war had been buried and
the trusting Malecites believed they had nothing more to fear. But, this
was not so.

One warm afternoon, Malabeam and her father stopped at an island
in the middle of the Wigoudi River. Sacotis pulled the canoe onto the
sand and went to his young daughter who was sitting quietly in the shade.
Malabeam smiled affectionately as he walked towards her. All at once, an
arrow zinged out of the bushes and the war-whoops of three hundred

Mohawks rang in her ear. Malabeam hurried to her father and tried to lift him up. But the arrow had pierced Sacotis' heart. He was dead.

The Indian girl fled in terror. But it was of no use, for she was surrounded by Mohawk braves. Their dark skin was plastered with war paint and they danced in circles around Malabeam and Sacotis, shouting chants of war. As they closed in, one of the warrior's siezed Malabeam's hands and feet, and tying them together with deer hide, he made her captive.

"You are our prisoner," announced the chief. "But your life will be spared if you do as I say. When the sun goes down, you will guide our war party to your father's village. Do this and your life will be saved and you will marry a Mohawk brave. If you refuse, you will be tortured and you will be made a slave."

"You have killed my father," replied Malabeam, "but I will guide you because I could never be your slave. You must bind your canoes together for the current is swift and broken. I will lead the way."

All the day long, Malabeam watched over the body of the dead Sacotis. And though her heart was sad, she shed not one tear. She thought instead, of how she might warn her people and save them from the treachery of the Mohawks.

When evening came, Malabeam slipped into her canoe and led the warriors down the dark Wigoudi towards the village at Grand Falls. When they had paddled for many hours, a noise like muffled thunder sounded in the distance. And as they approached the village, the sound became louder and louder.

"What is that?" called the chief.

"It is only a big flow of water which joins the Wigoudi down stream. Keep on," shouted Malabeam, "For the village is close by."

The warriors did as they were told. But soon they discovered that the river had become a raging torrent, which drove their canoes forward so swiftly it was impossible to stop or to escape. Malabeam looked back at them in triumph, her head held high.

"Come to your doom, Mohawk warriors," she mocked. "I will lead the way." With one final sweep of her paddle, Malabeam and her canoe disappeared over the precipice of the falls, into the black abyss. And down over the watery cliff plunged three hundred Mohawk warriors, to their death eighty feet below.

When the people of the peaceful Malecite village awoke next morning, they were astonished to find hundreds of drowned Mohawks strewn along the shore. Malabeam was not among them and her body was never found. But whenever men speak of brave deeds, they tell of how Malabeam sacrificed her life to save the people of her village.

Provincial Archives of New Brunswick

The precipice at Grand Falls.

Ke-Whis-Wask

Ke-whis-wask is known as Sweet Flag or Calamus Root, and is found by rivers and other marshy places in New Brunswick. The Indians have been using it for a long time and believe in its healthy effects. It is interesting to note that a group of Indians from California, when visiting the Passamaquoddy area, mentioned that they too used the calamus root for medicinal purposes and had done so for many years. The story was told to me by Dr. Peter Paul of Woodstock.

The Indians had a cure for just about everything, for they have had hundreds of years in which to learn how to use roots and herbs, animals and trees as medicines. But, many years ago, when the white man first came, the Indians became ill and began to die in great numbers. It was a white man's disease, so they didn't know what ailed them or how to treat it.

One evening, as an old Indian lay alone and sick in his wigwam, a stranger appeared. The visitor was an extremely tiny man, no bigger than a mushroom. He was one of the little people. He bent over the old Indian and touched him on the forehead.

"Are you very sick?" he asked.

"Oh yes, I am very sick," replied the Indian. "I am dying and so are my people."

"I can cure you." said the little man. "You must try to get up and follow me."

The Indian pulled himself together, and although he was very weak, he followed the little man down to the river's edge. The little person pointed to a patch of wide-bladed grass and said,

"Dig here and gather all the roots you can. Boil them in water and drink the juice. It will cure you."

The Indian did as he was told, and immediately the sickness passed from him. He was healthier than ever before. When his strength returned, the Indian made calamus root tea for all the people in his village and everyone recovered.

Since then, the tea made from calamus root has been used by the Indians, especially in the winter-time, to prevent colds and flu. In fact, it is used to prevent all kinds of illness and it is believed to make people live longer. The tea tastes like cloves, spicy and delicious.

The Little People

The "little people" are known by both the Micmac and the Malecite Indians as mythical creatures who wield considerable power. The Micmac name for them is "Megamawesu" and to refuse any request made by "Megamawesu" is asking for trouble. These handsome, finely dressed beings live in the woods and they can cure people with magic herbs and they are capable of transporting someone through the air.

Near New Mills in Restigouche County, I heard of an Irishman who had fairies living in his cellar. Otherwise, he lived alone, but at mealtime he set the table for five or six people, and opened the cellar door. When he ate, the fairies ate with him. People have spoken of fairy rings near Belledune and also around Sevogle which is where the following story came from. It was told to me by Ray Estey.

Remember the time they had the rebellion in heaven? Well, the angels flocked after the devil in millions and they're called "fallen angels" because they didn't hold up for God. Some are in the air, some are in the ocean and some are in the land. Fallen angels, that's what fairies be. They wanted to destroy the earth, but decided against it because they're hoping the Lord will take them back again and they'll all be saved before the end of time. That's why they don't do too much damage.

I'll tell you a story about fairies. There was a widow-woman and she lived all alone with her children in this big, beautiful house. The house was owned by a very rich man and she couldn't buy it because he wanted too much money for it. There was a fairy ring just outside her door, but she didn't know about it and she'd throw her dirty water out there right on top of the fairies. Damn near drowned them, I expect. So one night, a fairy came to her and complained. He said, "Look-it. You go and cut a door at the other end of your house and throw your slops and dirty water out there. We don't want you dumping it on us."

And the woman said, "Well, I'll do that, but what are you gonna give me for my trouble?"

The fairy told her to go down the cellar and to raise up a big, flat rock lying there. He said, "There's a crock of gold under it. All you have to do is take a handful of money out of the crock and put the stone back again. That'll make it yours. But don't let on how you got it."

The woman went down the cellar and lifted up the rock and, sure enough, there was the crock of gold just like the fairy said. She took a handful to make it her own and put the stone back. Then she went to the rich man who owned the house.

"How much do you want for the place?" she asked. "I'm very poor, but I'd like to buy it."

The rich man felt sorry for her and he let her have it cheaper than the original price. After she bought and paid for it, the woman boarded up the old door she'd been using and cut an opening at the other end of the house so she could throw her water out there. And that's the old people's story about how the widow woman got the house and all that money. She got it from the fairies.

And I'll tell you another thing. I used to have a grey mare and I'd groom her and comb her hair every single night. And every morning when I went to the barn that mare's mane was plaited from her ears right to her back. They were the prettiest plaits you ever did see and I swear you couldn't have put them in any neater yourself. There'd be ten or twelve of them and I'd have to take them all out. That's the fairies, you see. They won't go near any kind of horse but a grey one.

There used to be a fairy plot right out here and my grandparents would sit out on the verandah listening for them. Talk about nice music! They'd sit there for hours and hours listening to the dancing and fiddling and it was the lovliest music you ever heard!

The Man With the Cloven Hoof

There are lots of "cloven hoof" stories and usually the tales are told in response to a religious fear against drinking, gambling, fiddling and dancing or other "ungodly" pursuits. At Chaleur Bay I heard about a girl who went dancing against her mother's wishes and found herself dancing with a man whose hand was a cloven hoof. Another story revolves around a former dance hall near Shediac called "The Blue Circle" where the absence of a fiddler provoked someone to say "I'll get a fiddler if I have to bring the devil himself," and of course the fiddler left his mark behind in the form of hoof marks on the floor. All over the province there are stories about how gambling brought on the appearance of the devil and people in Buctouche have their own special version.

My mother grew up in Buctouche and she told me this story about the man with a cloven hoof. It seems that fishermen didn't make too much money in those days and they took to gambling, hoping to earn a little bit more. You didn't have to lose very much before it cut into the bread-basket for the wife and the kids. The priest wasn't too happy, but the men persisted.

They used to gather in a back room behind the bar in the old hotel. One night, this stranger walked in. He was tall and thin and he was dressed in black. He looked sort of familiar, but he was a stranger all right, because nobody knew who he was. He talked to them awhile about the gambling they were doing and eventually someone asked him to join the game, as a courtesy more than anything else. And so, he sat in. Immediately their luck turned sour and the stranger won quite a lot. He didn't take the money from anyone in particular, but apparently he won from each man in turn.

At the end of it, somebody protested and the game broke up. The stranger told them that if they wanted to gamble some more, he would be back to visit them again. He got up and walked out the door, and after he left, the men discovered the marks of a cloven hoof burned all across the floor. Jim Parry was one of the fellas who worked at the hotel and he was out "girling" that night. Jim was walking back along a road above the main street when he met the tall, dark stranger dressed all in black. It gave him quite a scare.

"Ai, yi, yi!", he said, "He was eight feet tall and he just stood and looked at me. And his eyes! 'Pon my soul, his eyes were blazing with fire.

He jumped sideways over a picket fence about six feet high, and I swear he cleared it by at least two feet!''

But, there is another side to the story. K.C. Irving had an uncle by the name of Jack and if ever there was anyone who liked to raise the devil, it was him. I knew the old buzzard well. He was about six feet, five inches tall and real skinny, so he looked even taller than he was. Some say that he and the priest got together and made the whole thing up. Others say that he did it on his own. Anyway, I'm not sure how he was rigged out, but he put some make-up on and he took a marked deck of cards to use in the game. If they'd of looked, they'd of seen that he didn't have hoofs to burn a mark on the floor. He had hoofs carved out of blocks straped onto the soles of his boots. He inked them and they left marks on the floor.

Meeting up with Jim was more than Jack expected. So, he did jump the picket fence, but it was only about four feet high. Jack was a long-legged fellow and at that time he was young and very agile. He stopped the gambling, that's for sure, and he gave them a mystery to talk about for the rest of their lives.

The School Master and the Devil

Many stories are told of that fascinating character, the Devil. Some stories tell how to make him appear, some explain how to get rid of him and others tell of his connection with books on black magic. This Acadian tale collected at Dupuis Corner in Westmorland County includes all three themes. It is adapted from a transcript in the Northeast Archives of Folklore and Oral History in Maine.

There were people living along the Atlantic coast of Canada who sold their souls to the Devil in order to receive supernatural powers, and many of the settlers who came from France brought with them large books on magic which had black pages with white printing on them and they were used to invoke the Devil. These evil books were called *"Les Livres d'Albert"* or *"Les livres de les Donés."* Naturally, the village priests were greatly concerned for their parishioners, and they went from house to house asking the people to surrender these black books for the good of their souls. When "Les Livres" were collected, the village held a great bonfire and the works of the Devil were almost destroyed.

But, there was a certain group of people who refused to give up their books, and they continued to practice black magic by dealing with the Devil and upon occasion they tried to show "Les Livres d'Albert" to others, hoping thereby to increase their numbers. Although the books were written in a strange language, all a person had to do was to pronounce the syllables written there and the Devil was sure to appear to take possession of the subject, if he were willing.

One night, a school master at Cocagne was sitting at his desk marking papers. It was very late, very dark, and very quiet and so he was greatly surprised when he heard a loud knocking on the schoolhouse door. He put his papers aside and opened the door and there standing before him on the steps was an old man holding a large black book. He thrust the volume into the school master's hands and said,

"Here. This book is for you, my son. Read it, for within its covers lies the key to a great power."

Before the school master could reply, the old man vanished into the night, and so the teacher carried the book to his desk and examined it. The pages were black, the printing was white and the language was one he had never seen before. Nevertheless, he began to sound out the syllables to see if he could make some sense out of it. After he had read one paragraph, he was stopped by another knock on the door. This time when he answered, he was greeted by a tall, pale man dressed all in black. The stranger's fiery eyes glowed like coals and he said in a hollow voice: "What is it you wish of me, Master?"

Immediately, the school master realized who his visitor was and he made the sign of the cross. There was a cloud of smoke and a great roaring of wind and the Devil disappeared. The terrified young man burned the evil book at once, and luckily for him, he was never again troubled by such visits.

The Wizard of the Miramichi

It is said that in the early part of the century, Ritchie's lumber camp on the Miramichi was deliberately burnt down after several of the men working there died of a mysterious illness. This story seems to be the centre from which other tales have grown, concerning a devious misfit called "Bill Lawless", or "Will Lolar." I collected anecdotes about him from Wilmot MacDonald of Glenwood, Chester Price of Priceville, Frank Munn of Storeyville and from a transcript of stories told by Harry Brown of South Nelson which I found in the Northeast Archives of Folklore and Oral History in Maine.

The legend of the Wizard of Miramichi was not told to me as the sequence of events which appears here. The story was collected in bits and pieces and I put the various fragments together into this particular pattern in order to create a continuous narrative.

Once there was a man by the name of Will who lived with his brother on a big farm near the town of Chatham. They didn't have a tractor or a baler or any of the heavy equipment that farmers use today, but that didn't matter because Will could do the work of a hundred men and a dozen tractors, if he wanted to. All he needed was his magic book and some help from his friend . . . the Devil.

One day, the brother rode into town on the horse and left Will standing alone in the middle of the hay-field. The grain was lying loose on the ground, so Will raked it up, bound the hay together in bunches, then waited for his brother to return with the horse so that together they could move the grain into the barn.

Suddenly, dark rain clouds gathered in the sky overhead, and it was certain that the crop would be ruined if it were not stored within the shelter of the barn at once. Quickly, Will reached into his pocket, drew forth his magic book, and began to read. And as he read, the air around him grew dark and heavy until it seemed as though the sun had burnt out and in its place a blanket of pitch was stretched across the heavens. The menacing moan of thunder crept nearer, then — crack! — the first prongs of lightning ripped across the sky.

Perhaps it was a signal, for at that very moment, Will leaped onto the old farm wagon. The wagon began to move by itself. It moved slowly at first, and then faster and faster until it was clattering down the field at a miraculous speed. Will stood on its wooden platform with his pitch-fork in one hand and his magic book in the other. Every time he rode by a bundle of hay, he shouted out some strange words and the hay jumped six feet into the air and landed on his fork. Before the first drop of rain had fallen, the field was emptied and the barn was stuffed to its rafters with hay.

When the brother came home and saw all the work that had been done, he couldn't believe his eyes. It wasn't long before the neighbours heard of Will's strange powers, and they told wild stories about him which spread all over the countryside. Nobody doubted that Will was in league with the Devil himself. Naturally, people began to avoid him, tradesmen would have nothing to do with him, and even his brother found excuses to stay away as much as possible. Finally, Will became so lonely that he decided to leave the farm and go to work in the lumberwoods.

There was a big lumber camp up on the South West Miramichi, and Will was hired on in the fall of the year and put to work chopping logs. Now, in those days, if a person chopped fifty logs in one day, he was thought to be a strong and mighty man. Will chopped one hundred and fifty logs every single day. At first, the men admired his studendous strength and they marvelled as his mountain of logs grew and grew. But no matter how hard the other choppers tried, not even the biggest and the strongest could chop as many logs as Will.

As months went by and the log pile grew, the men began to wonder. They watched closely, and they discovered that beads of sweat never appeared on Will's forehead, and he never got the least bit tired no matter how much work he did. The men thought for certain that he was in the Devil's power, and they became frightened and angry. They went to the boss and said,

"You'll have to fire that man or send him to work somewheres else in the camp. He's not like other men, that's for sure, and none of us want him around here!"

The boss was reluctant to lose such a good worker, so Will was asked to work as a funky, watering down the roads.

It was a cold, miserable job and Will's only companion was the young teamster with whom he worked. The teamster and his horse would drag a big tank of water out on two sleds while Will drew water from the tank with a barrel and splashed it over the road. It wouldn't take long to freeze, and then a heavy load of logs could be hauled over the smooth surface on a sled.

One day when Will and the teamster were swamping down the logging road, it came time for lunch. The teamster finished feeding the horse and then he said,

"We'll have to get some dry sticks and boil a kettle for some tea."

"No. No." said Will. "You don't need any wood to boil a kettle. Give that kettle to me."

As soon as the pot was handed over, it started to froth and bubble and boil, and flames flew forth from Will's hand.

"The Devil! The Devil!! I seen the Devil!!!" screamed the young man. And he was so frightened that he left his horse and his kettle and his lunch and streaked towards the camp. He didn't run very far before he had to stop, for suddenly it had become unbearably warm. A hush fell over the forest and everyone paused in their work to watch in amazement as the winter-grey sky turned to red and the sun blazed fiercely. The young teamster muttered fearfully and made the sign of the cross. Then he hurried to camp, gathered his gear together and left without a word.

Steam began to rise up from the river, hunks of snow slid down the trees and the men took off their heavy jackets and went back to work in their shirt-sleeves. The ice on the logging road melted, and when loads were hauled through the mud and slush, the horse's hooves and the sled runners gashed great holes and ruts into the soft surface of the ground. When it turned cold again, the ground froze up and the road was in a terrible mess.

"Look-it," said the boss, "we can't haul any more logs. We can't do anything till that road is fixed. You fellas will have to get out there in the morning and spend the whole day mending her up and swamping 'er down."

But early next morning, before breakfast, Will walked over to the boss and he said,

"Never mind fixing the road . . . Its as good as ever."

Of course, the boss thought that Will was joking.

"Go 'way with you," he said. "You just got out of bed, and you're still dreaming."

But, when they went out to look, the road was as level as could be, and as far as they knew . . . nobody had been near it.

"How could that be?" they asked, staring at Will. Will said nothing. And the men became more and more uneasy.

Then, another strange thing happened. Late at night when everybody was asleep, the whole camp would wake up to the sound of sleigh bells clinking and jangling in the distance. The sound became louder and louder until it reached the camp door. Then it would stop. About that time they were expecting a man to bring in supplies from the Company Store and that's who they thought it might be. But when they went out to look, there was never anyone there. No man. No horse. No footprints . . . Nothing!

"Somebody's playing a joke on us, thats what it is . . ." laughed the boss.

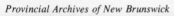

Lunch break at a lumber camp.

"No, it was a ghost. I swear t'was a ghost we heard! What else would make a noise like that and not leave any trace?" said one.

"Maybe its a forerunner. Maybe it means that one of us is going to die," said some others.

This went on for more than a week and the men didn't know what to think. Everybody in camp became very nervous, and in the end, they blamed the whole thing on Will. Again, they went to the boss:

"Look here," they said. "Either you'll have to let him go, or we're clearing out. There's been some strange goings on around this place, and it's all because of him. That man's possessed of the Devil, and we'll not stay in camp another day with the likes of that!"

By this time, the boss was a little upset himself, but it was his job to see that the work got done and that there was peace in the camp. He took the crew aside and tried to persuade them that Will was nothing more than a practical joker. And finally, the men were half-convinced that the strange happenings, even if they couldn't be explained, were just Will's queer way of having fun.

"If anything happens again," said the boss, "just laugh at him, and pay him no mind."

Once more, an uneasy truce was arranged between Will and the rest of the men. But it was not to last. In January the devilish powers erupted again. Will had been out swamping roads all day and when he came into camp, he said to the boys,

"Funny thing happened today. Awful funny thing. There was this big bird flying over me head all day, and it was talking to me."

"Oh yes . . . and what was it saying to you, Will?" they asked. "Was it a crow?"

"No, it wasn't a crow. Too big for a crow. Nor t'wasn't a raven either. It weren't really black anyway. He'd fly around and he'd light on a tree and he'd say, 'Beware of the night of the nineteenth.' Then bye and bye he'd land somewhere's else and he'd say it again. 'Beware of the night of the nineteenth.' "

The men tried to treat it as a joke. And every night when they came into camp they'd say,

"Well, its pretty near the night of the nineteenth, Will."

"I know," he'd say.

"Whats going to happen, Will? Something special?"

"I can't tell you," he replied grimly. "Wait and see."

Soon the appointed night arrived, a night very much like any other night. The sky was clear and the air crisp and cold. The woodlands and the lumber camp were covered in a silent shroud of snow. As the men entered the comfortable warmth of their camp, the familiar smells of fresh bread, molasses cake and wood-smoke greeted them.

"What could happen on a night like this?" they asked as they nudged one another and laughed.

"Well, this is it. This is the night."

"Yes," said Will. "I know it is."

"Everybody's well. Nothing wrong."

"Yes, that's right," he said.

The men got washed and when the cookee sung out for them to come and get their supper, they all went in and sat down. But suddenly they noticed they were one man short. A young fellow named Stuart was missing. The cookee went out to the men's sleeping quarters and he found young Stuart sitting there with his head in his hands.

"What's the matter?" asked the cookee.

"I don't know," he replied. "I don't feel like eating at all. Not now anyway. I just couldn't."

The cookee helped him into his bunk. The boy tossed and turned all night, burning with fever and suffering with headaches and a sick stomach. Some of the crew stayed up with him and carried water and held him down, when, mad with delirium, the lad fought to escape the strange demonic creatures which he thought assaulted him at his bedside. Despite all their efforts, nothing could be done and in the morning the boy was dead. His body was loaded onto a sleigh and sent home.

But, if anyone thought that was the end of it, they were mistaken. A few hours later, Cotton-tail John took sick and like young Stuart, the white-haired old man suffered terribly. When the sleigh returned, they carried him out, covered him warmly, and urgently prodded the tired horses to get him to the doctor. But before he travelled five miles out the road, the old man died too. One after another the men collapsed onto their bunks or dropped on the snow with the strange sickness. Many died, one man became stone deaf, and another lay flat on his bed for more than two years after that. The few who survived left camp, never to return.

The Board of Health in Newcastle sent Dr. Nicholson and several other doctors into the camp to see what was wrong, but there was little they could do. Their medicines had no effect on the disease, nor could they discover its cause. Some thought it was brain fever, others thought it was flu, but they never knew for sure. One thing was certain, the camp had to be burned down so that all traces of the sickness would be destroyed.

The man who owned the camp cried in despair when he learned what had happened. He had lost almost everything, and there was no way for him to get his logs moved down-river to the mills without a crew of men. All that remained were two big hovels where the horses had been kept, one of which had never been used. Finally, he decided to clean the horse's hovel and build onto it. Then he sent for new bedding, furniture and equipment, and he hired a new crew of men to come in and finish out the winter. Fortunately, there were no more deaths and the business was saved.

Will was one of the few men to survive, but he was the only one who offered to return to camp.

"No, said the owner. "I never want to see you again. You take your pay and get out."

"All right," replied Will. "Give me my money and let me go. But I'll tell you this. You're going to lose the best team of horses that you own."

And, sure enough, two of the owner's very best horses were drowned on the South West Miramichi that spring.

When Will left the camp, he walked into Chatham to get his cheque cashed at the bank. But when the cashier counted out the money, he accused her of giving him the wrong amount.

"You made a mistake there, didn't you?"

"I did?"

"Yes. You did."

She counted the money again, this time very carefully. Will had one hundred dollars coming to him, but when he left the bank he had enough money to choke an elephant. I don't know what he did with the money or where he went, but it must have kept him going for quite a while, because nobody ever heard tell of him again.

The Dungarvon Whooper

*People have been talking, singing and writing about the Dungarvon
Whooper for years. I heard the legend told by several people, including
Horace Hunter of Astle, Charlie Slane of McGivney and Irvine Van Horne
of Bloomfield Ridge. Some say that the whoops heard at Dungarvon are
made by the New Brunswick panther — a rare breed of wild cat which can
let loose with the most spine-chilling shriek imaginable. This cat has been
sighted in many wooded parts of the province and the northern area is one
of its favourite haunts. Be that as it may, almost anyone who has heard the
screams will say, "That was no cat!"*

A young cook by the name of Ryan hired himself out to work in a
lumber camp near the Dungarvon River. When he arrived at camp, he
brought all his worldly possessions with him. Instead of an alarm clock, he
carried a rooster in a bag to wake him up in the morning. He had a bottle of
yeast to make sourdough bread, and around his waist was fastened a
money-belt stuffed with coins and large bills. Nobody knew where he got
his money, but the young cook made no secret of the fact that there was
plenty of it.

Ryan was a handsome fellow. He was tall and strong with ruddy
cheeks and curly, black hair. Everybody liked and admired him, for not
only was he handsome and good-natured, but also he could whoop and
holler better than anyone in camp, and a good, strong shout was an
accomplishment much valued among woodsmen.

Every morning Ryan got up so early even the sun was still in bed. The
men he worked with slept under a forty foot long blanket on top of a bed of
fir boughs, so the young cook always had to ease himself out, careful not to
disturb his neighbours huddled close on either side. He prepared breakfast,
filled the men's lunchpails with bread and salt pork, then, let out a
tremendous earsplitting whoop.

Everybody woke up.

"Come on, boys. It's daylight in the swamp!"

The men washed and ate in the cold, thin light of morning, and as
usual, they tramped off to the lumberwoods, leaving Ryan alone in the
camp for the rest of the day.

It was an unlucky day for Ryan, for on this particular morning, the
boss of the camp decided to stay behind with the young cook. The boss was
a stranger, and although the men respected him and obeyed his orders,

A hunter with the pelt of a New Brunswick panther.

nobody knew very much about him. Maybe the boss was a good honest man, but, something happened that fateful day to make the woodsmen very suspicious of him. When the men returned late in the afternoon, they found their friend Ryan lying still and lifeless on the floor. He was dead and the money-belt was gone.

"What happened?" asked one of the men.

"Well," said the boss, "the youngster took so sick and he died so mighty quick, I hadn't time to think about what happened."

But, if he had died of a sickness, where was Ryan's money-belt? The boss had nothing more to say for himself. He would not explain, and none of the men dared accuse him of such a terrible crime.

That night, a raging storm swept down upon the camp, covering the ground with four feet of snow. It was impossible to get to town and there was nowhere to bury the poor cook, except in the forest. So the men took Ryan's body out into the howling blizzard and they dug him a shallow grave by the Dungarvon Spring. As they trudged sadly back to camp, the men stopped dead in their tracks. Above the howling and the moaning of the wind came the most dreadful whoops and screams that anyone had ever heard.

It continued all that night and all the next day, and the sound seemed to be coming from the Dungarvon Spring where Ryan was buried. The unearthly cries drove the men crazy with fear. They packed their belongings and left the camp, never to return.

For years, the Dungarvon was haunted by the sound of whoops which echoed throughout the forest and frightened everyone who heard it. And the hunters and fishermen who worked the Dungarvon were driven away from the haunted place. Finally, in desperation, they travelled to the village of Renous and knocked on Father Murdoch's door.

"Father," they said, "we cannot hunt or fish at Dungarvon anymore because of the screaming ghost. Can you do something about that poor murdered man and put his spirit at rest?"

The kindly priest shook his head doubtfully, but he said, "I will try."

Father Murdoch made his way through the wilderness to the Whooper Spring and stood over Ryan's grave. From his bible, he read some holy words and then he made the sign of the cross.

Now, some people will tell you that Father Murdoch succeeded in quieting the ghost. But, others will declare that the screaming still goes on and that the fearful cries of Ryan's ghost can be heard to this very day.

68

Whitlock's Ghost

The screams of the New Brunswick panther have been heard for years in different parts of the province and I wasn't surprised to find out that this animal appears in more than one ghostly story. The story of Whitlock's ghost was told by Robert Connors of Howland Ridge.

Those Whitlocks lived up here in a big house on the right-hand side of the top of the hill. One of the Whitlock boys went over to the Keswick on a stream drive and he took sick and he had to come home. He had pneumonia and maybe he had the TB too. But, he died at home.

At the time he died, there was a log jam at the Keswick Stream. The men who were working on the jam swore they seen this fella come upstream, walk around the log jam and then disappear. It was Whitlock. And he appeared at exactly the same time he passed away at home.

Quite a few years after, three fellas went over there to fish. They had a camp on the bank of that stream and they got their bunks all ready to stay for the night. It was in the summertime. And of course being boys, they took a gun along with them. It came along evening and one fella was friggin' around the camp and he looked out. He saw this man walking along the bank of the stream. It was on a bluff, way up high. I know the spot. I've been there lots of times. He said this man had on an old, long, dark coat and whiskers and high laced boots. And when he saw him comin', he said,

"Boys, there's somebody out there. Hide the rifle."

They stuck the rifle under the brush in the bunk and when they looked out again they saw that man walk right off the side of the bluff and they never seen him again.

Well, they got frightened then, and they thought they'd go home. It was comin' on pretty dark, so they lit this old lantern and they took this old rifle and they left everything else right there. They all lived at Millville, and they started for home. They got only a short ways when this great big animal jumped across their path in front of them. It was a New Brunswick panther, and you seldom see anything like that. It ran into the woods and took to screaming. They were deathly frightened, so they hurried and the thing jumped across their trail again. Johnny Gullison had the rifle, and he fired at it. It ran up into the woods, but it didn't cross their path again. It kept pace with them till they got pretty near to the clearing.

So, they went into Millville and got tellin' it around, and nobody would believe them. They had to get somebody to go back the next day with them to get their stuff . . . . their camping equipment. They wouldn't go back alone. They thought that the man on the river bank was Whitlock. And they figured it was a haunt.

The Red Haired Girl

I adapted the story of the Red-Haired Girl from a tale told to me by Frank and Ray Estey of Sevogle. These elderly brothers are regular performers at the Miramichi Folksong Festival, and they have a vast fund of stories which they love to tell. My husband and I sat by the wood stove in their comfortable kitchen from dusk until the wee hours of the morning, listening to them recall tale after tale about lumber camps, about moose, about bears, fairies and ghosts. Mostly, they talked about ghosts, and the stories are actually believed to have happened. As the night grew darker, and the stories became more serious and intense, I started to believe them too.

The story about Acadian treasure was told by Edward Jeffrey of Moncton.

There are many stories of treasure buried along the banks of the Miramichi, the Sevogle, the Caines and other rivers throughout the province of New Brunswick. Some of it is pirate treasure; some of it was buried in the earth by people who thought that the ground was a safer place than a bank. And some of it was hidden by the Acadians who chose to bury their valuables rather than lose them to the British who drove them from their lands many years ago.

There is one story about a man from Moncton called Mr. Melanson who liked to go fishing along the Memramcook River. On a hot summer's day when the fish were dozing and too lazy to bite at even the fattest and wiggliest of worms, Mr. Melanson got bored and decided that he, too, would take a nap. He grabbed his fishing pole and tried to shove it into a little hole in the side of the bank. But, the pole wouldn't go in because something was blocking its way. The man knelt down, peered into the hole and dug out an old iron pot which was full of coins. Mr. Melanson had found Acadian treasure and he suddenly was very rich.

Happily, for Mr. Melanson, this treasure wasn't guarded by a ghost. But if there is a ghost, it could turn out to be just about anybody. Take, for instance, the treasure buried near Wayerton. It was guarded by the spirit of a red-haired girl.

One night when old John Edmonds was fast asleep, he dreamed a very strange dream. He found himself sitting on a large rock, and seated opposite him on another large rock was the figure of a beautiful girl. She had long, flowing, red hair and her face was sad and unearthly pale. Old John stared at her for a long time, uncertain as to whether he was really asleep or in some kind of trance.

"Who are you," he said. "And what do you want?"

The figure turned to him and spoke: "There is a crock filled with money buried at Waye's bridge. If you go and dig it up, you will be rich. But if you want the treasure, you must first gather up my bones which are buried beside the crock. Go and bury them in the Presbyterian graveyard, so that I may rest in peace."

"How will I know where to dig?" asked John.

"I will tell you," said the ghost. "To the right of the bridge, there are two big rocks which are exactly six feet apart. The treasure and my bones are there. But, you must dig at midnight and you must go alone, or the treasure will be lost." And, with these words, the vision disappeared.

When John awoke next morning, he found himself alone and safe in his warm, soft bed. He thought that what he had seen the night before was nothing more than a silly dream. So, he went about his business much as before, and thought no more about it.

But, the next night, he had the same dream again. He found himself sitting on a large rock opposite the red-haired girl. Once more she begged him to dig up the treasure and to bury her bones so that she could rest in peace.

This time, when John awoke, he was puzzled and more than a little bothered by the night's happenings, for it seemed unnatural to have the same dream twice in a row. But, he didn't go to Waye's bridge. He was a little frightened and he didn't want to believe in ghosts anyway.

The following night, he had the dream for the third time. The girl sobbed and pleaded with him, and old John was so moved with pity for the young wraith that, against his better judgement, he agreed to do what she asked.

The very next night, John took his shovel, hitched up his wagon, and started for Waye's bridge which was a few miles away.

When he got there, it was almost midnight and he was beginning to feel not quite so brave as he did when he first started out. So, he stopped off to visit at the house of some friends. The house was up on a hill and was just a few hundred yards from the bridge. His friends wanted to know what was bothering him, so John told them about his dream and asked, "What do you make of it?"

They didn't know what to think, but they gave him some whiskey to get his courage up and told him to go and dig anyway. They promised to wait outside the house and to be ready if he hollared for help.

All too soon, the clock on the mantle began to strike twelve. Reluctantly, John picked up his shovel and ventured out into the blackness of the night with only a small flashlight to guide his path. It was quiet except for the sound of water trickling over stone and the moan of the wind in the trees.

He turned off to the right and stumbled around in some alder bushes until the beam of his flashlight flickered across a huge, white rock. There was another large rock just six paces beyond. The rocks were exactly like those he and the girl sat upon in his dream.

John put down his flashlight and started to dig. The ground was hard and gravelly, but he didn't have to dig long before he struck something. He reached down to lift it up. And to his utter horror, he found himself holding a human skull. He dropped the thing at once, and went to sit on a rock to steady himself. But there, sitting on the rock, was the same red-haired girl he had seen in his dream. She smiled at him.

It was too much for old John. He hurled his shovel and ran so hard you could have played checkers on his coat-tails. And when he got to the house he said, "I wouldn't go back if there were a hundred crocks full of money."

"Well, we wouldn't go either. Especially not at midnight, and certainly, not alone. But, the bones should be buried," said John's friends.

The next morning, everyone, except John, went to where the bones were buried and gathered them up. They were put in the Presbyterian churchyard. The ghost of the red-haired girl must have been happy, for she never appeared again. And as far as I know, the treasure is still there.

The Currie Mountain Treasure

Currie's Mountain is actually a steep hill which rises above the Saint John River above Fredericton. It is known for the unusual plants and flowers that grow there. The Malecites called it "Woo-cho-sis" and used the mountain top to guard against Mohawks, who threatened to raid their summer settlement at Hart's Island.

Currie's Mountain is not known as a place where treasure was buried, but maybe all that will change. I adapted this story told to me by Ralph Connors of Howland Ridge, and he says "it's as true as any story can be." The cannon which once may have contained gold stands in front of a farmhouse on the Keswick Ridge. It was rumoured that the cannon was found on someone else's property, and that this caused a feud between two families which lasted for many years.

In days of old, pirate ships sailed upon the high seas in search of vessels which carried gold, silver, or other valuable booty. The reputation of these pirate ships was so monstrous that even the bravest of sea-farers turned pale with fear when the word "pirate" was spoken. Many a ship's captain has been stopped dead at the end of a cutlass, and many a poor sailor has taken a long walk off a short plank and felt the cold brine of the sea closing over his head.

Pirate ships which cruised the Atlantic Ocean often sailed into the Bay of Fundy and buried their treasures along the shores of New Brunswick and Nova Scotia. Some sailed up the Saint John River in search of a good hiding place, and at least one pirate ship is said to have sailed up the river as far as a place called Currie Mountain. Nearby, a fabulous treasure was buried deep within the earth.

It was the custom in those days to leave someone behind to guard the treasure. This task usually befell some unlucky member of the pirate-ship's crew. Or, perhaps it would be a sailor who was taken hostage from a plundered ship. If a man was unfortunate enough to be chosen, he was shot or stabbed and then he was buried with the treasure. His spirit was expected to guard the treasure and to prevent others from taking the gold.

Sometimes many years would pass before the pirates could return, so they made a map to show exactly where the loot was buried. But, it often happened that the pirates themselves died before they could come back and recover the treasure and as a result, the maps were handed on from father to son and remained in the same family for many years.

Near Currie Mountain, there lives a certain family supposedly in possession of a treasure map, left to them by the pirate-king who buried his treasure near the mountain many years ago. But, strange as it may seem, nobody in the family has been able to find the gold. Two men have actually seen the chest, but they never did get their hands on it. Something strange happened to them.

It was midnight and the moon was full when the two young men set out to find the treasure. They carried with them picks, shovels, chains and the old map. When they found the spot where the treasure was supposed to be, they began to dig. They dug in absolute silence. They dared not speak a word, for to do so would awaken the spirit of the guardian ghost, and who could guess what might happen then!

They dug steadily and they dug for a long time. The hole got deeper and darker and they were getting tired and discouraged. But, suddenly, they heard a clink as the shovel hit something solid. One of the fellows got down on his hands and knees and began to brush the earth away. Soon, he could see the top of an old sea chest. Quickly, they dug out all around it, and then they tried to lift it up. The chest was very heavy.

They heaved and tugged and they pulled, but the thing wouldn't budge. Finally, the men wrapped their chains around it and they stood at the top of the pit and pulled as hard as they could. The chest loosened a little. Just as they gave one final, tremendous pull, one of the men forgot himself and groaned out loud. That did it!

As soon as the sound was uttered, a terrible vision arose from the depths of the pit. Before them appeared the ghost of a bearded pirate, with a cutlass driven clean through his stomach and out his back.

"Don't touch that," it snarled. "The treasure is mine."

The men dropped their chains and turned in fright. But, as they ran towards the river, their eyes beheld something even stranger than the ghost they had just seen. Out on the river stood a magnificent sailing ship, all on fire. The crew were running back and forth shouting and waving their arms while the rest of the men fired off the short, stubby cannons which lined the deck.

The treasure seekers were so scared, they stood rooted to the ground until, slowly, the vision of the phantom ship dissolved and the noise of the cannon faded away. With great caution, the men turned once more towards the pit they had dug. The ghostly pirate had disappeared. But, so too had the treasure. All that remained was an empty hole.

An experience like that might be enough to make most people give up treasure-seeking for life. But these two men were very determined. The sight of the treasure chest and the promise of all that gold made courage stronger than caution, and a few days later the pair set out again.

They did not go back to where they had dug before. And they did not go at midnight. Instead, they began to shovel earth out from under the corner of the local church. And, in broad daylight! For some reason, they were sure that the treasure had been moved there.

But good luck had completely deserted them, for they were stopped once again. Not by a ghostly apparition, but by a hoard of angry church-goers, who put an end to the nonsense once and for all.

So, the treasure was never found.

Or was it?

A few miles up river, a farmer discovered an old cannon half submerged at the bottom of a pond near his house. He dragged it up onto dry ground and cleaned it. And when he looked inside its broad barrel, he found that it was stuffed with golden coins. It was soon known that the farmer had great wealth, and he was envied by all his neighbours. If you drive by his house, you will see an old cannon standing there.

Was that part of the same treasure the young men were seeking? Or did pirates bury treasure all along that stretch of river? Maybe the gold is still there, waiting to be discovered by someone who is brave enough to dig it up.

The Burning Ship

Most people have heard about the Burning Ship of Chaleur Bay, and some claim to have seen it. Many versions of the story exist, but of the ones I found, I like this one the best. Maybe that's because I know that Gaspar and Miguel Corte-Real were real people. I can pick up history books and read about these Portuguese explorers who made voyages to Newfoundland, Gaspé and Nova Scotia in the years around 1500.

It is said that Gaspar Corte-Real discovered Newfoundland before John Cabot and historical records show he returned to Portugal with North American Indians for the slave trade. Gaspar's ship never returned to Portugal after a voyage to North America in 1501. When his brother Miguel set out to find him, he disappeared too, and both brothers were presumed lost at sea. That's where the recorded history ends and the legend begins. I adapted this version of the story from a description given by Ella B. Chase in In Quest of the Quaint, *Ferris and Leach, 1902.*

Gaspar Corte-Real was a very rich and successful trader and explorer who thought he knew how to get the best of any bargain. Every year his ship sailed up to Newfoundland and Gaspé where he gathered thousands of valuable furs which the Indians gave him in exchange for cheap trinkets, whiskey and guns. When the devious trader returned to Portugal, he sold the furs at a huge profit. Corte-Real did very well and his pile of money grew and grew. But the trader was a very greedy man and no matter how much he had, he was always looking for ways to get more.

After much scheming and conniving, Corte-Real had what he thought was a brilliant idea. He invited all the Indians to come on board his ship for a feast and all the liquor they could drink. The Indians trusted Corte-Real and they came willingly to join in the friendly feast. After eating and drinking a great deal, the drowsy natives were invited to sleep on board ship and to return home in the morning. But when they awoke, the Indians discovered that the ship was far out at sea. Corte-Real had them chained and stowed below deck for the rest of the long voyage, and when they arrived in Portugal, the unfortunate Indians were sold as slaves.

The venture was so successful that Corte-Real decided to try it again. He didn't dare go back to Gaspé, so this time he sailed up Chaleur Bay and anchored at Heron Island. He began a profitable trade with the Indians there who appeared to be very friendly. What Corte-Real did not know, was that the Indians had heard what happened to their friends from Gaspé, and all the while, they plotted to punish Corte-Real for this terrible deed.

One night when the moon was dark and hidden by clouds, the natives climbed aboard Corte-Real's ship and killed everyone but Corte-Real himself, who was saved for a very special punishment. They waited until low-tide, then took the trader and bound him tightly to a large rock. The Indians watched his agony as the tide crept in slowly and rose up around him, inch by inch. Finally, Corte-Real's miserable life ended when the determined waters closed silently over his tortured head.

Now, Corte-Real had a brother Miguel, who was himself both a trader and a seaman. He wondered what had happened to his missing relative and he set sail to find him. After two years, he drifted into Chaleur Bay and there, at Heron Island, he discovered Gaspar's ship. He was over-joyed and thought immediately how rich he too would become when the cargo on Gaspar's ship became his.

He and his men anchored beside his brother's boat and boarded it. But, as soon as they went below deck to look around, an angry swarm of Indians appeared. They leaped onto the vessel and killed almost all the Portuguese who were hopelessly unprepared for such an attack. Corte-Real and some of his men hid themselves in a cabin below ship. They barricaded the door with barrels and armed themselves with muskets they found stashed in a large wooden box.

Meanwhile, someone had hoisted the anchor and the ship began to drift out to sea. The Portuguese sailors knew that there was little hope of leaving the ship alive, so they joined hands and took a solemn oath. They vowed to fight to the end, to die together, and to haunt Chaleur Bay for a thousand years.

Corte-Real and his men deliberately set fire to the ship and rushed from the cabin, taking the Indians by surprise. A terrible battle took place as the ship burst into flames. Some of the men tried to save themselves by climbing up the rigging, but the ropes caught fire. Then, with a shudder and lurch, the burning ship sank beneath the waves, drowning all on board. Only one Indian escaped to tell the tale. When he was flung into the water, he found himself clinging to an old barrel which had rolled off the ship. He hung on and the tide carried him safely back to shore.

Forever after that, the ghost of the burning ship has appeared lurching up and down the Bay, from Dalhousie to Heron Island, Percé, and beyond. The Indians took fright when they saw the ghost vessel. They deserted

Heron Island and moved to the mainland. Fishermen still talk about the burning ship and many people who are alive today have seen it. They say that men can be seen on its deck, shouting, crying and climbing the rigging while the sails and the ropes and the spars blaze with fire.

Mystery of "The Union"

This story is adapted from newspaper reports, manuscripts and log-books, although I heard the story as a child. I've never heard an explanation about why the Union flipped over the way she did, but there are stories of ships along the Atlantic seaboard which have been upset in a vaguely similar way. According to sea-lore, it was possible to "buy wind" by throwing a coin overboard. Sometimes, if the coin was really a big one, the wind responded too enthusiastically and with disastrous results. Perhaps this superstition once formed a part of the Union legend, and was lost as the story was retold, but there is no real evidence to show that this is so.

Jack Dyre was alone in his cabin aboard the **Union.** He could hear the sound of waves scratching at loose rock on the shoreline, and once in a while, a seagull screamed, circled the barren masts of the schooner and then disappeared. It had been a long, boring day. The crew had gone ashore to visit their families at St. Martins and Dyre was left behind to keep watch. He had walked the deck and watched for sixteen hours, and how he was tired. He wanted to go to sleep.

The seaman yawned and mumbled to himself, "There's nothing here to look at but the stars and the night and the sea. Time for bed."

He turned down the blankets of his bunk and curled up for a long, peaceful night. In the distance, the lights of St. Martins went out one by one and the **Union,** tugging gently at her moorings, rocked slowly back and forth like a giant cradle. Soon, Jack Dyre was asleep.

It was just past midnight when a strange voice awakened him. He sat up in his bunk and heard this command:

"Jack Dyre. Leave this ship."

Jack lit his lantern at once. He looked all around, searched below deck and above, but couldn't find anyone. Finally, he returned to his cabin.

"I must have been dreaming," he said as he rolled over and drifted off to sleep.

The voice awakened him again:

"Jack Dyre. Leave this ship."

Jack jumped up, lit his lantern and made another search. But, again, he found nothing which would explain the eerie voice. It seemed certain that nobody was aboard the **Union** but himself. Nevertheless, his voice shook with fear as he repeated to himself,

Sailing ships at St. Martins.

"It was only a dream . . . only a dream . . ." Soon, his head drooped down on his chin, his eyelids closed and he began to snore. But, once again, he was rudely awakened:

"JACK DYRE. LEAVE THIS SHIP." This time the voice was loud and angry and insistent.

It was more than Jack could bear. He did not bother to search. He didn't even bother to light his lantern. He just threw his clothes in a bag, fumbled around in the dark until he found the ship's companionway and escaped from the schooner as fast as he could. The crew of the **Union** found him at dawn, pacing the dock at St. Martins. Shivering, pale and hollow-eyed, he clutched his seaman's bag to his chest and waited for Captain Kelly to approach.

"What in the name of heaven possessed you to spend the night here?" roared the captain.

Jack explained as best he could.

"Aw, come on Jack. You've been having nightmares. We're sailing for Shulie this morning to pick up that load of lumber, and we need you on board. Pull yourself together, man!"

"No sir. I won't," replied Jack. "I will never set foot on board the **Union** again. Never!"

"Alright, lad. Suit yourself," said the captain. "Bill Bradshaw is looking for a job. I'll hire him to take your place."

It was a beautiful, clear day and the Captain set sail at noon. The **Union** drifted on the tide for awhile, steering for Shulie, Nova Scotia. She got part way across the Bay of Fundy, then stopped. There was no wind to carry her further. The **Union** and forty other ships waited in the Bay outside St. Martins, with their white sails reflecting on the mirror-like surface of a calm, unmoving sea.

The afternoon wore on, and Captain Kelly kept glancing at the sky, praying for a change in the weather. Clouds were gathering overhead and it looked like rain. But there was not a whisper of wind on the Bay.

"Put on your oilskins mates. It's going to pour!" called Kelly.

At that moment, the **Union** was plucked out of the ocean like a toy and then she dropped, with her bottom up and her sails down. One of the crew had just stepped on deck when the schooner turned upside down. He leaped from the side and swam towards the ship's keel and hung on. Captain Kelly was trapped below in the galley. He forced open a hatch, dived into the companionway which was under water, and then surfaced a few feet from the **Union.** The two men managed to crawl up onto the bottom of the ship. They clung together in the pouring rain and called out to their companions. There was no reply but the steady beat of heavy rain on still waters.

By early evening, the rain stopped and a team of rescuers rowed out to the capsized vessel. They took Captain Kelly and his mate to shore. The **Union** was pulled right side up, towed to St. Martins, repaired, and safely sailed the Bay for another twenty-eight years.

Who's voice did Dyre hear? And how could the **Union** flip upside down without wind or waves to turn it over? Nobody knows. The story of the **Union** is one of the many unsolved mysteries of the sea.

The Keswick Valley Ghost

I adapted this from a story told by Professor Robert Cockburn in his office at the University of New Brunswick. Bob heard the story from the people who lived in the house.

Among the many beautiful old homes in the Keswick Valley, there is one house which was abandoned and remained empty for a long time. Nobody would live in it. In fact, many people were afraid to go near it. On dark nights, a strange amber glow could be seen moving from window to window in the upper part of the house, and those who saw the ghostly light were convinced that the place was haunted.

The building stood vacant for many years, until one day, a young couple came from far away and they looked at the old house and decided that they liked it very much. They found much to admire in its unusual structure and in its gracious rooms and in the large expanse of field and forest which surrounded the property. When they discovered that the owner was willing to sell the place at a very low price, nothing could dissuade the young couple from buying it. And when the people of the valley came to warn them that the house was haunted by a ghost, the man and his wife merely laughed. They did not believe in such things.

As soon as the couple moved in, they began to paint and make repairs. They put in new plumbing and wiring and they sanded the wooden floors and waxed them and they spent all their money renovating the place. Soon the house looked as splendid as it did when it was first built more than a hundred years before. It was a beautiful house, and the couple were very happy there. Many months went by, and there was no sign of anything that remotely resembled a ghost.

But one day in July, something unusual happened. A small pane of glass in the upstairs window suddenly and inexplicably smashed into thousands of small pieces. The window appeared to have been shattered from the inside. Neither the man nor his wife had been near the window when the pane shattered, and there had not been anyone else in the house at the time. They investigated both the inside of the house and the outside, and in the end, they still could not explain why the window broke the way it did. But, after a while, they stopped talking about what had happened and eventually they almost forgot about it.

However, the following year on the very same date, the glass broke again. It was smashed from the inside. Again, nobody had been near the window when it broke. And for some mysterious reason, the same window continued to break on the same date, year after year. That was the first thing that happened.

Then, a few years after they moved into the house, the wife began to have a dream. She would dream the same dream over and over again. In her dream she saw a man on horse-back riding past the house towards the bank of the river. The man was dressed in an old-fashioned uniform. It was the kind of outfit that a British Army Officer could have worn a century before. He wore a military jacket which was bottle-green in colour, and he had a three cornered hat decorated with a badge of some sort. His trousers were white and they were tucked into a pair of kneehigh laced moccassins. The man's face was pale and distraught, and in the woman's dream he would always turn to her and declare, "I didn't do it! I didn't do it!"

The wife had this dream several times a year, and the dream recurred so frequently it began to bother her and she became very curious. Who was the figure in her dream? And why was he so distressed?

The couple began to question the people in the valley, and they were told many things. One of the stories they heard appeared to have some connection with the dream.

It seems that at one time the house in which they lived was used as a resting place for soldiers and wayfarers who travelled between Quebec and Fredericton. Travellers could get a meal there and sometimes people stayed overnight. It happened that the paymaster for the British Regiment stationed in Fredericton had to make the journey from Quebec City, and he had in his possession a large amount of gold which was to be used to pay the soldiers of the Fredericton Battallion. It is likely that he had a number of guards with him for protection, because it was very dangerous to travel the highways alone with so much money. Often people were beaten and robbed for much less than the fortune in gold he was carrying with him.

It was a long and tiresome journey by horseback, so the paymaster and the rest of his company decided to stay the night at the house. Then, in the morning, they would travel the eighteen miles into Fredericton. But, the paymaster never finished his journey. That night he was murdered and the payroll was stolen and nobody knows whether or not the murderer was caught.

After she heard this story, the wife felt fairly certain that the figure in her dream was one of the guards and that he had been wrongly accused of the crime. She thought that the words, "I didn't do it," which he repeated so often, were perhaps a desperate plea to convince someone of his innocence.

But there was one thing which puzzled the woman. In her dream, the road which the man on horseback travelled ran by the side of the house and along the river bank. And the side of the house and along the river bank was all grown up in trees and bushes and there was no sign of a road there now. Not a trace of one. Finally, she and her husband located some old maps of the area, and they discovered that the original road was exactly where she dreamed it had been. Both the man and his wife were strangers to the Keswick Valley, so neither of them could have known about the old road. And yet, in her dream, the wife had seen the landscape as it was more than a hundred years ago when the murder was supposed to have taken place.

About ten years ago, an old woman came to the door of the house. She had been absent from the Keswick Valley for forty years, but she had grown up in the house and she asked if she could see it again. The young couple were willing to oblige and they showed her through all the rooms, and they took her to the attic at the top of the house to the cellar at the bottom. Just as she was about to leave, the old woman turned to the wife and she whispered,

"Have you ever seen IT?"

Of course, they had never actually seen anything, and so the wife replied, "No . . . What do you mean?"

The old woman didn't answer. Instead, she hurried away from the house, and the young couple were puzzled.

But, one summer when the wife was upstairs taking a nap at two o'clock in the afternoon, she awoke suddenly and saw a strange shape standing in the doorway. She couldn't tell whether the shape was that of a man or a woman, but it seemed to be an amber colour. She decided to go to the door to see who or what it was standing there, but as soon as she got up, the shape disappeared.

Since then, neither the man nor the woman have seen or heard anything else. But, right to this day, the wife continues to have the same dream. And, the same window pane continues to break regularly on the same date, every year.

The Residence Ghost

A few years ago, Professor Judith Kennedy of St. Thomas University and I went to the Boyce house, a student residence located off-campus, to interview one of the students living there. The story of the Residence ghost was told to us by a young man who had seen the apparition himself.

On Waterloo Row in Fredericton stands a large Victorian-style house painted a dark, sombre grey. It was built by a gentleman named Boyce more than seventy-five years ago. A few years ago the house was used as a men's residence for students attending the University of New Brunswick, and the students complained of another inhabitant, an ethereal creature who stole their mail, played the piano, moved desks and drifted up and down the staircase and in and out of rooms.

The Don of the residence was a young man who'd had some religious training in the Anglican Church and he slept downstairs next to the recreation room. One night he awoke to the sound of the piano playing and he was very annoyed about having his sleep disturbed.

"Hey, you guys," he yelled. "I don't know which one of you idiots is banging on the piano, but don't you know what time it is?" But, the piano kept playing, so the Don crawled out of bed and headed for the next room. As soon as the piano came into view, he could see that no one was there. And the playing had stopped.

Shortly after that, the same fellow passed a strange woman walking down the stairs. She seemed slightly unreal and since he didn't know her, he asked, casually, "What are you doing here?" There was no answer and when he turned to look at her again, he realized that the creature wasn't made of flesh and blood. The Don summoned up his courage and addressed the apparition:

"In the name of the Father, the Son and the Holy Ghost, I command you to tell me who you are and to state your purpose."

To his immense surprise, the ghost replied that she was looking for a letter. She wanted him to open a safe in the kitchen to see if it was there.

The problem was that the kitchen appeared to have no safe in it. Nevertheless, the students believed there was some truth to the story because their own mail had been tampered with. Letters which were left on the table in the hall disappeared mysteriously and in their place were found quarters and dimes and other small change. It was thought that a ghost had something to do with it. They tapped on the kitchen walls, looking for a clue to the missing safe and eventually they found it behind some panelling which had been installed when the house was renovated. The safe was locked and it was necessary to send away for the combination. A few months later, they opened the safe but the letter was not there.

The lady continued to wander about the residence and was especially active just after Christmas during the "mid-term slump". One of the students recalled his experience:

"Three years ago, I used to stay in the master bedroom on the second floor, and it was then that I first saw her. Well, actually, I didn't see her the first time, I just heard her. I was lying in my bed which was by the door, and the door was locked. I turned the key in it myself. I heard the door open and I heard footsteps go right past my bed and over to the balcony door on the other side of the room. My room-mate woke up just then and he saw the balcony door open and close. It was three o'clock in the morning and everybody on the whole floor seemed to wake up at the same time. Bill and Don were in the next room to us. They kept a dog and when it woke up, it started barking and chasing around their room. All of us went out to the kitchen on our floor and started talking about what had been happening".

"It was my first year in the house and I hadn't heard about the ghost until then. After about twenty minutes, I looked up and this time I actually saw her pass by the kitchen door. I didn't believe it! What I saw wasn't what I expected to see. I suppose you could describe it as being like the energy that comes across on a television set. It was white and strong and formed in a definite human shape and you could see the head, the shoulders, the waist and the legs. It didn't take too long to walk by, so I couldn't do a total appraisal, but it was like a mass of energy and I have no idea what she was wearing because she disappeared too quickly."

Later that month, one of the boys who lived alone on the third floor had a nerve-wrecking experience. He had his desk in front of a storage door which led out under the eaves of the house. He entered his room after returning from classes and saw that the desk had been moved away from the door and the door was left open. He assumed that while he was away someone went into this room because they wanted something stored under the eaves. So, he just closed the door and pushed the desk back. He went into the washroom and when he came back the desk was pulled out and the door was open.

The boys in the residence thought the lady haunted the house because she was looking for an important letter she never received. The present owner has suggested that the woman may have been grieving over a son who died when he was a young man and she wished to be around other young people like him. Whatever the reason, her visitations are confined to boys in residence.

Rescued from Purgatory

I adapted this story which came from a collection in the Northeast Archives of Folklore and Oral History, University of Maine, and was told by a Sister of Charity in Saint John in 1965.

During the Depression of the 1930's, jobs and money were very scarce. But there was a young girl in Saint John who always saved one dollar out of her weekly pay to have Mass said for some poor soul in Purgatory. Every week she went to the Rectory at the West Side of the city and arranged with the priest to have this done. She kept it up for many months.

The time came, however, when the factory where she worked was forced to close down and the girl was dismissed. She came from a poor family and had no money of her own except her one week's wages which was, in itself, very little. Since she had lost her job and every dollar was so precious, the girl was tempted not to pay for the Mass as she usually did. She debated with herself about what to do. At last, she decided to go to the Rectory and have the Mass said anyway. She left her boarding house and walked to the bus-stop to get over to the West Side. While she was waiting here, a man came up to her and said,

"Do you need a job?"

Of course the girl was delighted and she said, "Yes," immediately. The stranger gave her an address to go to and he told her she would find work there. She thanked him, and after she left the Rectory, she went to find the house where the man had told her to go. It was a stately, imposing home and when she rang the bell, a maid answered the door.

"I was told I would find work here," said the girl.

The maid looked puzzled. "There must be some mistake," she replied. "There are no jobs here."

The young girl was flustered and embarassed. She started to turn away, but, just before the door closed behind her, a woman's voice called out from the back of the house: "Who is at the door?"

The maid answered, "It's a girl looking for work."

"Send her in," said the woman. The girl was shown into the room where the woman was sitting. It was a luxurious room with red velvet curtains, oriental rugs and ornate mahogany furniture, but the first thing the girl noticed when she entered was a photograph on a desk over by the window, and she exclaimed: "Why, that's the man I met at the bus stop, the one who told me to come here."

"But, that can't be," the woman protested. "That's my husband who has been dead for twenty years."

They both looked at each other in amazement, and after the girl told her story, the woman explained that her husband had not led a christian life. They reasoned that the Masses the girl had paid for helped rescue his soul from Purgatory and the husband was showing his gratitude by sending her to his wife for assistance.

Unfinished Business

This story was told long ago by Parks' wife who told it to Frank Estey's mother. His mother told Frank and this is how Frank told it to me:

On the south side of the river here, down below Red Bank, there was a man named Parks. And on the other side of the river, right across from him, lived a man named Williams who came from England. They were great buddies. Parks would go to Williams' place and Williams would go over there and for two or three years they were real friendly. But, Williams took sick and died.

He was dead about six months or so when Parks took off for a walk one night and the first thing he met was Williams.

"Oh, Hello Williams," he said, forgetting that he was dead.

"I'm so glad you spoke," Williams said. "I want you to do something for me."

It was then that Parks realized Williams was dead, and he said "I don't think there's anything I can possibly do for you, but if there is, I'll do it. But if I can't, I can't."

"Don't worry. There's nothing to it." answered the ghost. "I just want you to write a letter for me."

"Sure, I'd write a letter for you," said his friend. "But the thing is, I ain't much of a writer and I don't spell too good."

"Well," Williams said, "never mind. You bring your pen and paper and I'll help. I'll tell you what to put in that letter and you'll find you can write just as good as I can."

So finally, Parks said, "If that's the case, I'll do it. But where will I meet you?"

"There's an old blacksmith's shop right across the road. Meet me there."

"Will I take a light?"

"No, don't do that. I'll furnish the light."

Parks went right home and he told his wife all about it and she said, "You're crazy! I wouldn't take a million dollars to do a thing like that." But Parks told her that he'd given his promise and if he didn't keep it "I'll probably meet up with him again."

Anyway, when it got good and dark, Parks picked up his pen and ink, went to the old blacksmith shop and stepped up to the door. "Are you there, Williams?" he called.

"I'm here. Come right in."

Parks went inside and it was just as black as pitch. Williams held up his hand, like that, and everything lit up. It was brilliant. He had something that looked like a candle in every finger.

"Shut the door," he said. Parks shut the door. He spread out his papers and uncorked the ink and they started at it. Williams wanted his business in the old country fixed up and he wanted to leave something to this relative and that. Finally the ghost told him,

"That's everything. You put that in the envelope now. Seal it and stamp it and mail it tomorrow."

Parks told him, "I certainly will." Then, they sat back and they talked about everything on this earth, just the same as if Williams was living. But pretty soon it got to be near twelve o'clock, and the dead have to leave before midnight, you know. Parks said to his friend,

"There's one thing I want to ask you before you go, How are ya doin' in the next world?"

Well sir, there was an awful expression came over William's face and his looks changed something fierce. But he kept his lights on. He said, "Oh, Parks! Why did you ask me that? The dead aren't allowed to tell anything. That's the secret of the Most High . . . . , And if we wasn't such buddies I'd tear you to pieces right now!"

Parks said no more, but he got up enough courage to just whisper, "Well, I didn't know."

"That's all right," Williams told him. "You'll never see me again. Now be sure to mail the letter and I'll take you to the door."

As soon as Parks got to the door, the lights went out and it was as dark as the inside of a black cow.

When he got home, his wife said he couldn't have been wetter than if he'd swum the north-west river. He was sweating so, the water ran right out of him and she had to change his clothes twice that night before the man could lie down. See, if you promise a ghost anything, you've got to do it. If you don't, they'll haunt you to death. Parks died the very next year. Ain't that incredible?

Telling tall tales at Camp Comfort.

Yarns and Tall Tales

Is That You, Charlie?

Tall tales are often told as a humorous reaction to hardship and disappointment. They are popular throughout North America, including New Brunswick. These outrageous falsehoods are usually told in a matter-of-fact tone with the speaker keeping a straight poker-face. The listener is supposed to accept these stories as fact, and he should try to reply by telling an even bigger and better lie. I've heard of Liar's Contests which went on all night.

I'm willing to bet that Charlie Slane of McGivney could give anyone a good run for their money in any of these competitions. Charlie used to work in the lumberwoods when he was a young man and he spent many summer evenings around the campfire as a scout leader. He's had some remarkable experiences . . . especially with bears.

Did I ever tell you the story about the bear I had one time? I guess most kids would like to have a pet of some kind. And, more than anything else in the whole, wide world, I wanted a pet bear. This friend of mine told me that if he ever trapped a female bear, and if the female bear had a cub, he'd bring the cub to me and let me keep it. And that's just what he did.

It was late spring when I got the bear cub from him, and it was just the cutest little thing you ever saw. It was black and furry with bright, brown eyes. I called him Charlie. Charlie lived with us for about two and a half years, and he grew into a big handsome bear. He used to sleep in the barn in the hay-mow in the winter. In the summer he occupied our front porch.

I was always trying to teach Charlie tricks. But you know, it's a hard thing to teach a bear tricks and a bear is not like a dog. He might be half as smart but he's twice as stubborn. So, the only trick I ever taught him was to haul this little cart I made for him. The cart was made out of wood and it had a harness on it so I could hitch him up and he'd haul that cart along just fine. He really seemed to enjoy it. I used to take him back in the woods while I chopped down trees. I'd cut the tree up, put the logs in the cart, and Charlie would haul it home.

Well, like I said, Charlie often slept on our front porch, on the step right outside our door. We never let him in the house because bears can't be housetrained. But when I got up in the morning, I'd nudge him with my toe to wake him up. He'd always get up and lick my hands and rub against me and ask to have his back scratched. Bears like their backs to be scratched, and I always did that for him.

But one morning, when I went to wake Charlie up, he wouldn't budge. He just sort of lay there and growled down deep in his throat. So, when he wouldn't move like he was supposed to, I gave him a good kick to get him going. And you know, he got right up on his hind legs and snarled at me. It was unusual for Charlie to snarl at me because he was always such a good-natured bear. In fact, he didn't act like the same bear at all.

So, I gave him another good kick in the ribs. I throught, ''I'll teach you not to talk to me like that!'' And Gee Willikers! Didn't he snarl at me again, and paw at me too! So, I grabbed him by the scruff of the neck, jerked him off the front porch, and gave him a couple more thumps. I figured he had to learn just who was boss, before he got too darned ugly.

When I tried to put him into his harness, I had one heck of a tussle. Normally, he liked it, but this time he didn't seem to want to go. I had to drag him into the woods with the cart and when I did get him back there, he didn't want to stay.

Well sir, I cut up the wood and put the logs in the cart and started to wrestle with the bear to get him to haul the logs back. I had to grab him by the ear. Bears don't like to be grabbed by the ear because it hurts. But anyway, I grabbed him by the ear to pull him along. It wasn't easy, I tell you. He snarled and pawed and fought me all the way.

Finally, I got within sight of the house. I could just see the porch from where we were standing and what I saw scared me so much, my hair stood on end. For there, curled up on the front step was the real Charlie, dozing peacefully in the sun.

The Friendly Bear

*Bears have always been a hazard in the lumberwoods. They break
into camps to steal the food, and as everyone knows, they can be pretty
ferocious in the spring. If, like Charlie, you can get a bear working for you
instead of against you, then you've got it made.*

One time I was working in a lumber camp and I was out in the camp
yard splitting wood for the cook stove, when I saw this bear. Bears like
hanging around camps because they pick up scraps and garbage and that
type of thing. This bear came out of the trail from back in the woods and he
went behind the cookhouse. So, I followed him to see what he was going to
get into. He was a good-sized bear.

We had these old puncheons back there which at one time had been
filled with molasses, but they were pretty well empty. There was always a
little molasses left inside them, of course, because you could never get
them all cleaned out. So, the bear went up to the barrel and he hauled out his
fist and he banged in the top of it. He smashed it right in. That's hard to do,
you know. Even if you smash one of those things with an axe, you have to
hit it about a dozen times before you can break through. But, he just
thumped it once, and the whole top caved in.

He reached in with his paw, way down to the bottom of the barrel
where the molasses was and he got his paw all full of molasses. Normally,
the first thing a bear would do is to eat that sticky, gooey stuff, because they
just love molasses. It's sweet, just like honey. But, he didn't eat it. He got
his paw full of it and started off with his one paw held up and cantered away
on his other three legs. I thought I'd better follow him to find out what he
was going to do.

Right in back of our camp was where we'd get our water. It was a fair
sized stream called Clearwater Brook. Well sir, the bear waded out to the
middle of the brook to where there was a big rock, and he went and sat on
that. Then, he held his paw out over the water, just three or four inches
above it.

This was in summer, and the flies began to swarm all around his paw
which was covered with gooey molasses. Then, suddenly, a trout jumped.
It was after the flies, you see. But, when the trout jumped, the bear took his

other paw and went WHOOSH — and grabbed the trout and threw it up on the bank. He did that about eight or ten times, till he had almost a dozen trout piled up on the bank.

Then he stopped and he looked over to where I was. I was standing on the bank, peeping out through the alder bushes. He saw me and he grinned. Then he held out his big paw and went Whoosh — plunk! Whoosh — plunk! Whoosh — plunk! and tossed me enough trout for my supper. Now that's what I call a friendly bear.

A Catch Tale

Be careful if you hear this story. It's a "catch tale." A storyteller like Charlie Slane will try to lead you on and trick you into asking him a question. Then, when he answers, you'll discover that you've been hoaxed.

You don't see bears around as often as you used to. But I remember seeing one once when I was out picking raspberries. It was the end of August and it was hot. It was a real scorcher! And there I was, down on my knees, making my way around the raspberry canes. Suddenly, I came nose to nose with this great, black bear.

He was doing the same thing, of course. He was eating the raspberries, stripping them off with his big paw and stuffing them in his mouth. He was surprised and annoyed that I was picking his berries, because he growled and got up on his hind legs. Well, I didn't hang around.

I took off down this old woods road, and when I looked back, he was coming along after me on all fours. Bears can run pretty fast. I can run pretty fast too. I was running the mile in about two minutes, at least. But so was the bear and he was right behind me.

I ran and ran and ran. It was awful hot. The sweat was just pouring off me. I'd look back every once in a while, and the bear seemed to be getting a little closer. So, I put on a little more effort and I ran for an awful long time. I was getting tired too. But the bear was still coming on. He wasn't getting any farther away. In fact, he was just as close as he could be.

So, I ran and ran and ran. I ran for an awful long time. And just when I thought I couldn't run another step, I came to this lake. It was frozen over a little bit. There was just an inch of ice over it, and I knew that it would hold me if I ran over it real fast, and I knew if the bear followed me, it wouldn't hold him.

So, I ran out onto the ice, and I stopped in the middle. And there came the bear, charging after me. He paused for a minute when he saw me out there, then he ran right out on the ice. He got just about halfway when the ice cracked and gave way and down he went and drowned. That was the end of him.

"Hey! That can't be true. You said it was summertime and awful hot. There wouldn't be any ice on the lake then!"

"Yup, it's true all right. It was summertime when I started running. But, like I said, I ran for an awful long time."

Lucky Dick

This is one of the biggest whoopers I ever heard, and Horace Hunter from Astle told it to me. Horace used to work at lumbering and trapping. He writes poems about local activities and family events, he knows countless stories, makes his own dancing men and plays the harmonica. His story about Lucky Dick is a masterful exaggeration.

There used to be an old homestead on the Miramichi called The Palmer Place. Some say it's still standing, but I've never seen the place for myself, so I couldn't say for sure whether it's still there or not. They had just about everything they needed except a grindstone.

If you wanted a grindstone in those days, you had to get in your boat and pole the boat about fifty miles down the river to a place called Quarryville where there was a great mountain of rock. One of the hardest jobs of all was prying the rock loose and getting it in the boat, because sometimes the rock would have to be about the size of a bathtub, which is pretty big. Then, when you got the thing loose, you had to knock off all the edges and smooth it down and sand away at it until it was perfectly rounded. Then you'd have to bore a hole through the centre. To make a grindstone took a lot of time and a lot of patience. But that's how things were in the old days; if you wanted anything, you usually had to work very hard to get it.

There were two brothers living at The Palmer Place and their names were Geordie and Dick. Dick was famous for his good luck. Wherever he went and whatever he did, things went well for him and if there was good fortune to be had, it always landed right in Dick's lap. Geordie liked to go everywhere with Dick because Dick was so lucky. So, when the family needed a grindstone, there was no question about who should be asked to get it. They asked Dick.

Dick's mother packed a big lunch and Geordie went along with Dick to keep him company. The two of them got into the little boat and started off down the river. They were poling along near Quarryville when the sky started to cloud over. But Geordie and Dick kept right on going until they reached the rock quarry and they moored their boat in front of a great mountain of rock.

Well, then, it started to rain, and it rained something fierce. The raindrops were so big they looked just like pebbles falling out of the sky, and the water splashed up so that Geordie and Dick got soaking wet. The two brothers sat in their little boat waiting for the rain to stop.

But, the rain didn't stop. It kept right on pouring, and there came a tremendous clap of thunder which was so loud, it shook loose a gigantic rock at the top of the mountain. It began to somersault down the cliff. The rock was at least as big as a bathtub, and it was headed straight for the boat where Geordie and Dick were sitting. As the rock thumped down the mountain, its edges began to chip off, and the further it rolled, the rounder it got, so that by the time it neared the bottom, the rock was perfectly rounded.

Then, a chain of lightning streaked across the sky. It made a right turn, spun around, zipped down, and struck the huge stone in the middle making a neat hole right in the centre of it. Of course by that time, the rock had reached the bottom of the mountain and it landed in Dick's boat just as easy as you please.

With the edges all chipped off and rounded and with the hole in its middle, that big, shapeless rock had been turned into as good a grindstone as any man could make in a couple of weeks.

Dick was feeling pretty lucky, because all he had to do now was to take the grindstone home. He poled his boat around. But, just as he was starting off, a big tidal wave came rolling up the river. It picked up the boat with Dick and Geordie and the grindstone and it carried them right up to the front door of The Palmer Place. And that goes to show you just how lucky Dick was.

How The Bear Got His Short Tail

According to Chester Price of Priceville, there was a time when a young fella couldn't even get a girl if he didn't tell bear stories and Chester knows lots of stories about bears. Whenever How the Bear Got His Short Tail *is told, there are usually two main characters: a wily fox who uses his fine skill and a foolish bear. But this adaptation of Chester's story shows that some bears are so clever they can fool themselves without any help at all.*

If you look at a bear closely, you'll notice that he has a very short tail. It wasn't always like that. In fact, the bear's tail used to be long and bushy and magnificent, as far as tails go. What happened to the bear's tail is sort of sad, but I'll tell you about it anyway.

In the middle of winter, a long time ago, the bear became very hungry and decided to catch some fish. He crawled out of the cave where he'd been sleeping and went off into the woods to look for the river. Of course, the water in the river had frozen over and was covered with ice, but this didn't stop the bear, because he was ravenously hungry. He began to paw away at the ice, and pretty soon he scratched a hole so deep it reached right down to the water underneath.

Well, he couldn't see enough of the water to catch a fish with his paw, and he didn't own a fishing rod, so he decided to use his magnificent tail.

"Surely," he thought, "the fish must be just as hungry as I am, and my tail looks so nice they won't be able to resist it."

The bear stuck his tail into the hole and sat down on the ice and waited. He waited for a very long time. But, nothing happened. He was a very patient bear, though, so he sat there all day and all night. Finally, he thought,

"I guess the fish don't like my tail, after all. Maybe it would be better if I tried something else."

He started to get up. But, to his surprise, he found he couldn't move. His tail had been in the river so long, the water had frozen over it and he was stuck. He pulled and he twisted and he grunted and he heaved. And after one final desperate effort, the bear managed to wrench himself loose. But, when he looked behind him, he saw that his beautiful tail was still stuck in the ice and all that remained on his poor backside was a wretched, insignificant, little stub.

To this day, the bear has had to make do with a short tail instead of the long one he lost so very long ago.

Chester's Trout

Chester Price likes to tell stories "on himself" and he has won many Liar's Contests as a result. I think he even beat Tom Hunter once, and I think he must have done it with this story.

When I was just a young lad, I went fishing on the river which runs past my front door. What I caught was a tiny trout, no bigger than your little finger. Since it was too small to eat and too weak to return to the river, I decided to keep it in the well at the back of the house.

So, down it went and there it stayed for a number of years. I was so busy trapping and tanning skins I forgot about the little fellow. But one day when I dropped the bucket down the well, there was this big fish hanging out of the pail. The tiny trout had grown up. It had grown too big for the well and I could hardly contain it in the bucket. I took the fish down to the river and I let it go.

The trout didn't go very far. It was used to swimming in the well, and all it could do was go around in circles. I felt sort of responsible for the fish, so I sat on the bank and watched it for a while. I wanted to make sure that it would be all right.

After a time, I looked up and saw a big, hungry-looking fisher-hawk roaming around the sky, searching for food. Suddenly, the hawk caught a glimpse of my trout, and dove down to pluck it from the water. I thought my trout was a goner, for sure. But, as soon as the hawk got near enough to follow the trout, the bird began to go round and round in circles. It got so dizzy, it just dropped into the river and drowned.

Pretty soon, another hungry fisher-hawk came by. It saw the trout. And when it tried to follow the fish, the hawk went around in circles until it, too, plunged into the river and drowned.

At least ten fisher-hawks perished that afternoon. And after that I lost count. Anyway, I stopped worrying about the trout because the trout could look after itself. I began looking after fisher-hawks instead.

A Fishing Yarn

Anglers love to tell fishing yarns and I heard several of these stories told around the Saint John River, the Miramichi and the Restigouche. Chester Price told me this one, but I also heard it from his nephew Allan Wilson and from others who fish the Miramichi.

These two fellers were great fishermen and every time they met they started in telling fish stories. They got together one day and one of the fellers said,

"I caught a fish here just a few days ago. I had it on my line all day and all that night, and when daylight came next morning, I landed it. That salmon measured twelve feet in length. Do you believe that?"

The other guy said, "Sure. I believe it. But I had an experience a few days ago which was very different than that."

"You did? Well, tell me what happened."

"Well, I hooked something. I couldn't tell what it was and I couldn't bring it in. Finally I got it towed down river a piece. I got it in the quiet water and clear of the rocks and I dragged it to the shore. It was an old oil lantern and it was lit. It was still burning! Do you believe that?"

The other feller said, "Well no. Not quite. I don't believe all of it. It's mostly just a story because a lantern wouldn't still be burning under water."

The guy said, "Well look. I tell you what I'll do. You take nine feet off your salmon and I'll blow the lantern out."

Up a Tree

William Harris of Bloomfield Ridge told me this story. He used to own a hunting and fishing lodge on the Miramichi. I never did find out whether it was one of Mr. Harris's guests who ended up in a tree, but whoever it was, he must be glad that beavers aren't what they used to be.

This fella was out moose hunting one time and he came upon a big moose standing in a clearing. Before he could get his gun out to take a shot, the moose charged after him. The fella was so surprised he dropped his gun and ran as fast as he could. He climbed up a big beech tree, and he made it just in time too, for the moose was right behind him. Once he got up there, he hung on tight because the moose started butting that tree and shaking it, trying his darndest to get him down.

This went on for quite a long while and the fella thought he'd never get away. Finally, the moose took off towards a beaver pond and the hunter started to climb down. He got half-way down the tree when he stopped to look around. He saw the moose coming back and the moose had two beavers with him. They were going to cut down the tree. The hunter figured that was the end of him. But anyway, he climbed back up the beech tree and he stayed there. The moose looked up at him and said:

"I'm gonna get you!"

The man stared right back at the moose and he said, "Ha! Those are pretty old beavers and this is a mighty big tree!" But if the truth be known, that fella was feeling very uncomfortable up there.

The beavers chewed and chewed all morning and all afternoon. The tree was beginning to creak and bend. But then, all of a sudden the beavers stopped chewing. They looked at each other; they nodded, and then they walked away.

It was five o'clock and they belonged to the Union, you see.

The moose was disgusted. He shook his head and mumbled, "Well, I'm gonna get you *sometime!*" Then, off he went dragging his antlers between his knees.

Shingling in the Fog

The fog up around the Miramichi Bay gets pretty thick sometimes. Whether it's caused by mists from the Miramichi River or by the pulp mill is difficult to say. William E. Spray of Chatham told me this story to explain just how bad the fog can be.

It was a foggy day, and since I had nothing to do, I thought I would go and call on my friend, Arthur. He doesn't live very far from me, so I pointed myself in the right direction and started off down the street. Soon, I found myself in front of something which seemed like a door. I couldn't see very well on account of the fog, but, it felt like Arthur's door, so I knocked.

"Who's there" said a soft voice.

"It's me," I replied. "I'm looking for Arthur."

"He's out back, working on the garage," said the voice.

"Thank you," I said, and I made my way towards the back yard. The fog was so thick, I couldn't tell where the garage was until I bumped my nose on it.

"Arthur," I called. "Where are you?"

"I'm up here," came a muffled reply.'

"Up where?" I asked.

"I'm up here on the roof."

"What are you doing up there, on a foggy day like this?"

"I'm hammering shingles on the roof."

"What?" I said. "Shingling the roof in this fog? How can you see?"

"Oh, I can see well enough. I think."

Since Arthur is such a good friend of mine, I decided to stay for a while and keep him company. We talked for a bit, but then, the fog got so bad I couldn't even hear his voice. So, I just sat on the ground and waited for him to finish.

Several hours passed, and it seemed to be taking an awful long time. I couldn't see or hear Arthur at all, and I began to get worried. I thought something might have happened to him.

But, all of a sudden, the fog cleared. And there was Arthur, six feet out from the end of the roof . . . . still shingling!

The Big Mosquitoes

I used to spend my summers on the Bay of Fundy near Alma, and I always thought the mosquitoes down there were something wicked. But, according to William E. Spray of Chatham, they can't be compared to the ones flying around Grand Dune Island, near Bartibogue.

There can't be anyplace in the world where the mosquitoes are as bad as they are around here. I was out picking cranberries with a friend of mine, and I spent all of my time just swatting and fanning the air trying to get rid of the pesky creatures.

"My heavens, the mosquitoes are bad!" I said.

"Look-it," replied my friend, "They aren't nearly as bad as they were last year."

"Gee," I said. "They must have been mighty ferocious if they were worse than this last year. Were they big?"

"They were big!" said my friend. "I remember coming down here to pick cranberries, like we're doing now. And the first thing I knew, I heard this loud rushing sound. I couldn't tell what it was, at first. Then I looked, and I saw a great, black cloud of mosquitoes coming right for me.

Lucky for me, I found a tar-pot which someone had left lying on the shore after they'd finished tarring their boat. So, I lay down on the sand, pulled the tar-pot over my head, and got into it. I figured I could get away from the mosquitoes that way.

I wasn't inside the tar-pot for more than a minute when I heard a sound like hail, hitting the top of the pot. When I looked up, there were these mosquitoe stingers coming right through the metal. I had a rock beside me, so I picked it up and as fast as those stingers came through the pot, I hammered them down just like nails.

The next thing I knew... Whoosh! Away flew the mosquitoes carrying the tar-pot, with me inside it.

Now, if you can tell me about mosquitoes bigger than that, you'd be telling a mighty tall tale!"

The Fable of the Three Frogs

Eldon Green is a well driller in Astle, and he and his cousin Horace Hunter like to get together once in a while to swap stories. I was lucky enough to be invited to one of these sessions held round the table in Mrs. Green's kitchen. The Fable of the Three Frogs is one that Eldon told, and I often thought of the moral of this story whenever I felt bogged down with collecting, transcribing and writing.

While I was visiting at a farmhouse, I was asked to fetch a kettle full of water at the spring. When I walked down, I discovered this big, wooden cream pail sitting there beside the spring. It was full of cream, but the cover was off. Sitting beside the creamer were three little frogs. They were croaking away, just as happy as they could be.

When the frogs saw me, they jumped. And they jumped so high, all three of them landed in the creamer. I watched them to see what they would do.

They splashed and kicked and thrashed around, but they couldn't seem to get out. Finally, two of them decided it was hopeless. They both gave up trying and they sank to the bottom and drowned.

But, the third frog kept at it. She paddled and churned and paddled some more. The cream got thicker and thicker. Finally, she paddled such a long time that a pat of butter started to form on top of the cream. The frog climbed up on the chunk of butter, and gave a mighty hop and got out.

And that just goes to show you that if you try hard enough and long enough, you'll get the job done.

The Ghost of the One Black Eye

Folklore is everywhere. It can be collected in kitchens and offices, and from children as well as adults. Crystal Arnold heard this "Shaggy Dog" story on the playground of the Marysville Elementary School. She told it to my son Michael, and Michael told it to me.

A family was sitting around the kitchen table one morning, when the baby started to cry.

"Waa...waaaa! I want my apple juice. Waaaa...!"

"Don't cry, baby," said the baby's big sister. "I'll get you some juice. It's down cellar." So, the big sister went down the cellar steps and when she got to the bottom, she heard a deep voice which said:

"I-Am-The-Ghost-Of-The-One-Black-Eye!"

"Yikes!" cried the sister. And she ran back upstairs. "I can't get your juice, baby. There's a ghost down there!"

"Wa..waaaa! I want my apple juice. Waaaa..!"

"Boy! What a coward!" said the baby's big brother. "Don't cry. I'll go and get it for you." So, down he went, and when he reached the bottom, he heard a deep voice saying:

"I-Am-The-Ghost-Of-The-One-Black-Eye!"

"Yikes!" exclaimed the brother. And he ran up to the kitchen as fast as he could. "I can't get the juice," he said. "There really IS a ghost down there!"

"Waa..waaaa! I want my apple juice. Waaaa..."

"Oh, for heaven's sakes!" said the baby's mother. "I'll go." She opened the cellar door and went down. And when she got to the bottom, she heard this:

"I-Am-The-Ghost-Of-The-One-Black-Eye!"

"Yikes!" cried the mother, as she turned around and came dashing up the stairs. "Sorry, baby," she said. "You'll have to wait."

"Waaa..waaaaaa! I want my apple juice. Waaaa...!"

The mother turned to her husband and said, "Why don't you go, dear?"

"Why not," said the father. "I don't understand what all of this fuss is about anyway!" The father went down cellar. And when he got to the bottom, he heard a deep voice which said:

"I-Am-The-Ghost-Of-The-One-Black-Eye!"

"Yikes!" he yelled. And, quick as a wink, the father came back to the kitchen. "Sorry," he said. "No juice."

"Waa...waaa! I want my apple juice. Waaa....!

"Well," said the father, "you'll just have to wait till tomorrow when we go shopping. I'll get some then."

"Oh, never mind," replied the baby. "I'll get it myself," The baby crawled down the cellar stairs, and when it reached the bottom, the deep voice began:

"I-Am-The-Ghost-Of-The-One-Black-Eye!"

"QUIET!" shouted the baby. "Or I'll give you another black eye!"

"Yikes", said the ghost. And he ran away.

Jimmie Willie

Jimmie Willie Fitzgerald was a local character around Newcastle and people just naturally told stories about him. They say when he first came to North America he landed in Boston where his brother met him. In Boston, they saluted the setting sun with a blast from a cannon, but Jimmie Willie didn't know this. The cannon went off so loudly it nearly brought the clouds down.

"What in the name of heavens is that?" asked Jimmie Willie.

"That's sundown," said his brother.

"Well! Don't it go down with a jeez-less bang around here!!" replied Jimmie Willie.

Frank Estey told the following story:

Jimmie Willie was a real comical fella who was always getting in trouble. He was out travelling the woods one time and he got awful tired. There was an old forsaken house way back in a field somewhere and Jimmie Willie decided he'd go there and lie down for a bit. No one had been living in the house for a long, long time.

So he went in and found an old horse-hair sofa sittin' right next to a door leading up the stairway. He took off his old boots, put them beside the couch and lay down and went to sleep. He slept for quite a little while, but a loud noise woke him up and he heard something at the top of the stairway say,

"Just you and me!"

Jimmie Willie sat up and listened and he heard it coming down the stairs, one step at a time.

"Just you and me!" it said, and it was getting down to the bottom of the door.

Jimmie Willie put one old boot on and he heard the door latch click at the end of the stairs.

"Just you and me!"

Jimmie said, "Say fellow. Let me get this other boot on and, by heavens, it will be just you!!"

He struck out for the country road and he could feel the hot puffs coming right down the back of his neck. There was a jack rabbit in front of him. And you know how fast a jack rabbit can run . . . . about twenty feet to a jump! Well, Jimmie Willie booted him in the behind for about five miles and finally he told him, "Get out of my way and let someone run that can run".

The Haunted House

This is another version of almost the same story. I've included it to illustrate how different the "same story" can be. This was told by Horace Hunter of Astle.

There was this haunted house in the settlement, and it was a beautiful house too but no one could ever stay in it. It was deserted and they offered the place to anyone who could stay there overnight. They could have it! A lot of people tried, but no one could ever stay there because there was always something that would scare them out before morning. So, this fella went to see the parson to see if he could persuade him to go there with him and stay the night. And the parson said,

"Sure, I'll go with you".

It was in the fall of the year and the weather was starting to get a little cold. So they went. They got into the house and they put a fire on in the fireplace. The parson had his bible and he read a chapter out of the bible while the other fella took a chapter out of his bottle. Oh, everything was goin' smooth. No noise nor nothin'. They were talking together and by and by they heard heavy footsteps upstairs. It said,

"Look out, I'm comin' down!"

They heard these footsteps and the parson opened the door and ran out onto the highway road. And he ran about half a mile up the highway road with his coat-tails stickin' right out, and the other fella was right behind him.

The parson said, "Do you s'pose the Lord is with us?"

The other fella said, "Boy, if he is, he's sure travellin' ".

Dan McCloud and the Ducks

Dan McCloud worked as a cook in the lumber woods, and as a local character he was known for his wit. Several stories have been told about Dan, and Horace Hunter told me this one about Dan and the Ducks.

This is a story of Dan McCloud. He was quite a lad to hunt and he used to like duck hunting awful well. One time he went out hunting on a little lake. It was only a small lake and it was almost perfectly round.

He crept up pretty close to the lake and he looked out and sure enough there was ducks clear round the lake right in close to shore.

He just had one shell for his shotgun but he wanted to get as many ducks as he could. So, he went back in the woods a little ways and he hit the barrel of the gun across a tree. He struck it right in the middle and put a bow in the barrel. Then, he went out to the lake and he fired. He said he got ninety-nine ducks with one shot.

Someone said, "Gosh Dan, why didn't you make it a hundred?"

"Huh!" he said. "I'll be damned if I'm gonna make a liar out of meself for one duck!"

Geordie Brown Stories

Wherever I went around the Miramichi, people would tell me stories about an old trapper called Geordie Brown. I checked the census records and discovered he was born in Tracadie of Scottish parents in 1825. He lived to a ripe old age and is buried in an unmarked grave in the United Church graveyard in Boiestown. Geordie spent most of his life trapping in the woods between Renous and Boiestown and once in a while he helped out at a lumber camp. He lived a solitary life, he never married, and he became well known as a lovable eccentric. The Sheriff of Northumberland County constantly hounded him for non-payment of school taxes, and in 1877, the law finally caught up with him. Geordie landed in jail in Newcastle because he owed the county one dollar and thirty-two cents. When he was very old, Geordie sometimes boarded at different houses along the river. But when he died, they say he died in the woods, with his boots on, his body resting peacefully against the trunk of a tree.

There was this rich man whose partner ran away and cheated him out of twenty thousand dollars. So, the rich man found himself in reduced circumstances. His wife had never learned to cook, and when she was compelled to start cooking, she made an awful mess of it. At that time, there was an old trapper boarding at the house and his name was Geordie Brown. The woman made pancakes for breakfast one morning, and the pancakes weren't very good. She made the mistake of asking Geordie if he liked them.

Geordie said, "Well, I have eaten a lot better ones".

She wasn't too happy about that remark and she replied, "Humph! You ought to be glad to get them".

"Well," said Geordie, "I might see the day when I'd have to eat them, but I wouldn't be glad".

That got the woman really riled up. "You might chase a crow a mile for one of them pancakes, come spring".

"Ha!" said Geordie. "If I did, t'would be to save the crow's life!"

(*Harding Smith, Fredericton*)

116

Geordie used to build these dams for the Richards Lumber Company. One time, one of Geordie's axemen got sick and had to go home, so he sent out word to young Bill Richards to send him in a good axeman. But Bill Richards didn't send him in. Geordie had to work short-handed all the time he was building the dam, and of course he didn't like that too well. Geordie wasn't too particular what he said to these Richards because the Richards didn't care what you said to them so long as you worked all day and half the night. So, Geordie came out to the lumber office after he was all done building the dam, and he said to Bill Richards, "Why didn't you send me in an axeman?"

"Well," Bill said, "I couldn't find one".

"What do you mean, you couldn't find one!" says Geordie. "There's lots of good axemen in this country".

By this time, Bill was getting a little mad himself and he said to Geordie. "There was no axeman around here. And I couldn't *make* a man!"

"No," said Geordie. "And your father couldn't either!"

Young Bill Richards used to tell that story to everybody who came in.

(Harding Smith)

Geordie Brown was a man who used to drink a lot, and he liked nothing so well as a bottle of whiskey. So, Herb Gunter who worked for the Richards Lumber Company, went and got a bottle of strawberry fruit syrup. He wrapped it up in paper and he came in and he crooked his finger and he said, "Come on back here, Geordie." He made a great secret of it, and Herb took Geordie down to the back of the store and gave him the bottle and he told him, "Don't you open that until you get on the train."

Geordie thought it was a bottle of whiskey. But, of course if it had been a bottle of whiskey, perhaps Herb Gunter wouldn't have given it to him. But anyway, when they got on the train, Geordie met an old crony of his and he said, "Come on out back on the platform with me. Come on, and we'll have a drink."

So, this old feller went back with him, and Geordie took the cork out of the bottle and handed it to him. The feller took one taste of it, and he said.

"That ain't whiskey. That's fruit syrup."

Geordie took the bottle and he threw it down on the railway track and he broke it. He declared that there were only three big liars in Boiestown. Bill Richards was one, and Herb Gunter was the other two.

(Harding Smith)

Geordie Brown, the trapper, at a camp near Boiestown.

Old Geordie Brown got drunk at Duffy's Hotel, which was down there where the garage is now. Geordie was so drunk, he decided he'd better stay at the hotel all night. So Charlie Duffy led him upstairs and told him,

"You'd better get into bed, and I'll cover you up."

But Geordie just stood there, looking at the bed.

"What's the trouble Mr. Brown?"

"Charlie," he says, "the next time that bed comes round, I'm gonna board it!"

(Irvine Van Horne, Bloomfield Ridge)

One day Geordie was sitting in the lumber store. There was a sign posted up on the wall. It said that they didn't want anyone to spit on the floor. A man came in, bought a plug of chewing tabacco, and when he noticed the sign he said,

"You sell chewing tobacco here?"

The owner said, "Yes, we do."

"But you don't allow anyone to spit on the floor? That's strange."

Old Geordie was sittin' right there, and he spoke up, "Yaas, they sell Epsom salts here too!"

He was witty, Geordie was.

(Harding Smith)

There was a man who wanted to learn how to trap, but he was a very simple-minded feller. So, he asked Geordie to tell him how to set traps so he could catch different animals. Geordie told him,

"I don't think you need any trap."

And the feller said, "My gracious! Don't need a trap? Why wouldn't I need a trap?"

And Geordie said, "Any animal stupid enough to let you catch him could be caught without a trap!"

(Harding Smith)

Geordie had a camp on a lake near Rocky Brook. They called it Geordie Lake, and t'was named after him. All he had was a smoke-hole up through the roof, and he took cataracts on his eyes from being in the smoke so much.

They say he used to trap saple and bobcats and lucifees. One time, he caught a saple, and a lucifee ate the saple right out of his trap. So, Geordie set a trap and he caught the lucifee. He kept that lucifee in the trap for a long, long time. He cut a stick and went back to the trap every day and beat the lucifee. He said,

"That'll learn ya to sit up at night and eat saple!"

(Harding Smith)

119

One time, Geordie was in the woods trapping. He got a little behind in his taxes, so they sent the sheriff in after him. The sheriff told him he would have to take him to jail if he wasn't able to pay his taxes. So, Geordie reached in behind the door and picked up an old gun he had there. He said,

"Did anyone see you come in here?"

The sheriff said, "No, they didn't."

"Well," Geordie told him, "if you don't move pretty quick, nobody's gonna see you go out either!"

(Eldon Green, Astle)

Geordie Brown was a great trapper, you know. And one of the stories they used to tell, was about the time that he killed a bear. He had this little camp in the woods, and he arrived there one night to find that a bear was in it. Geordie didn't have a gun or anything, so when he heard the bear in there, he went out and he got a piece of firewood about four feet long. He went in and he met the bear, face to face, and he killed that bear right then and there.

Sometimes he worked at a lumber camp, and the men used to get him telling stories. They got after him one night and they said,

"Geordie, tell us how ya killed the bear."

But, Geordie always had trouble telling stories because he stuttered. He said,

"Well, I c . . . c . . . c . . . come to my c . . . c . . . c . . . cabin, and - "

"Never mind, Geordie," they said, "Show us, Show us how you killed the bear."

Geordie went out and picked up a piece of wood. It was the kind of wood they used in barrel stoves and it was about three feet long. He picked up a club of that wood and he said,

"I c . . . c . . . c . . . come in l . . . l . . . l . . . like th . . . th . . . this . . ."

The men had a feller there they had rigged up like a bear. And Geordie just hauled off and smashed him. And down he went.

And someone said, "Good heavens, Geordie! What are you tryin' to do? You pretty near killed that man!"

"Well," said Geordie, "He was the b . . . b . . . b . . . bear, and I was Geordie B . . . B . . . B . . . Brown!"

So, they didn't fool with him no more. He was gonna be Geordie Brown, and he *was* Geordie Brown!

(Clarence Curtis, Newcastle)

120

When Geordie got pretty old, he used to stay up at the Fairley house on Taxis River. One day, he told Allen Fairley that when he died, he didn't want to be buried. So Allen says to him,

"Look here, Geordie. You know we'll have to bury you. Everybody gets buried around here."

Geordie said, "Well, if you do bury me, I want you to bury me in a hemlock casket."

"A hemlock casket? What's your reason for wanting to be buried in a hemlock casket, Geordie?"

"Because," said Geordie, "Hemlock snaps and burns real fast, and when I get to hell, I want to go through there snappin'."

(Frank Munn, Storeytown)

Geordie used to come out of the woods in the summertime and he'd go and board with old Mrs. Spencer. She was awful good to him and she'd knit him five or six pairs of socks and five or six pairs of mitts to keep him warm in the winter. She said to him one day,

"Geordie, do you go way into the head of Rocky Brook and Dungarvon and Renous and all those places?"

"Yaas," says Geordie. "Same as I always do."

"And do you go all alone?"

"Yaas," says Geordie. "Same as I always do."

"Well," said Mrs. Spencer, "you're gettin' pretty old, Geordie. What are you gonna do if you die in there?"

"I'll do what any dead man would do," says Geordie, "Stay put!"

(Harding Smith)

Ken Homer, right, Master of Ceremonies, introducing singers at the Miramichi Folksong Festival. From left to right, Harold Whitney, Wilmot MacDonald, Stanley MacDonald and Ken Homer.

Recitations

Woe Unto You, Ye Bocabecers

Woe unto ye Bocabecers
Ye Hansons and ye Turners
You think more of your logs
Than you do of your God
You wouldn't come out of the woods
To bury your old father.

There shall be a bear
Come and devour you
Not one of those little black bears
That roam the Bocabec hills
But a great bear
With jaws of iron and teeth of brass

(Hill Brownrigg, St. Andrews)

"Woe unto you, ye Bocabecers" is a friendly greeting still heard in the area around St. Andrews and usually the phrase is addressed to the people of Bocabec, Charlotte County. Dr. J.D. Medcof of St. Andrews has done considerable research into the origins of this folk phrase and he discovered that it comes from a diatribe delivered in the 1850's which has survived for more than a century. There are several versions of the diatribe and of the story which prompted it.

According to the most commonly acceptable story, the Hanson and Turner men were working in a lumber camp when the patriarch of the Hanson family died. The journey home from Forest City would have been a long and arduous one and so the Hanson women decided to make the funeral arrangements themselves without the men in attendance. The minister was most unsympathetic towards the situation and during the course of the service he launched into a diatribe which has never been completely forgotten. It has been suggested that the text which inspired the outburst comes from the second chapter of Kings where two young men are chastized for failing to honour Elisha.

Another more modern and fanciful version states that the women decided to await the men's return and stored the body in the woodshed for the winter. But, before the burial could take place, a rodent deprived the patriarch of his nose and this state of affairs inspired the preacher to vent his indignation in no uncertain terms. The "curse" has travelled to other parts of the province and has been attached to other families besides the Hansons and the Turners. Dr. Murray Young of Fredericton says he remembers he was about twelve years old and sitting on top of the old Mount Hope fire tower in Penniac, York County, when he heard a variant of the diatribe delivered by a young playmate whose mother came from Charlotte County.

The following was composed by Dr. Medcof as a "possible version" based on the many different variants of the diatribe he has found.

> *Woe unto you, you Bocabecers!*
> *You Hansons and you Turners,*
> *You deserters of heaven,*
> *You think more of your logs*
> *Than you do of your God.*
> *You wouldn't come out of the woods to bury your father!*
>
> *She-bears slew Bethel's children*
> *Who mocked the prophet Elisha.*
> *Tremble you now before God*
> *You who dishonour your dead!*
> *Tremble lest He send a great bear to tear you*
> *With jaws of iron and teeth of steel*
> *And take you down into his bowels*
> *And from there into hell and damnation!*
>
> ("Woe Unto You Ye Bocabecers", by Dr. J.D. Medcof in *Collections of the New Brunswick Historical Society*, No. 19, 1966)

The Days of Duffy Gillis

"The Days of Duffy Gillis" was written by Hedley Parker, who was born at Derby, Northumberland County in 1856. He later became Marine Editor on a newspaper in New York where he wrote the poem in 1899, and then he sent it to the Miramichi Advance. *It was natural for Parker to write in the old ballad tradition because the "Come all ye's" were the sort of narratives he'd heard all his young life. "The Days of Duffy Gillis" was not traditionally sung in the lumber camps probably because Parker wasn't there to sing it for them and it is rather long. But it did catch on as a poem and people at Miramichi have been reciting it for years. The poem vividly expresses the quality, the speech and the rhythms of Miramichi life.*

The Days of Duffy Gillis
(A Lament in G Minor)

Come all you jolly lumbermen
  Whose better years have fled,
And I will sing of halcyon days
  Before we had Confed.
When two logs made a thousand,
  Our country at its best,
In the days of Duffy Gillis
  From the Sou-ou-West.

When title to respect was writ
  Upon each horny hand,
And the man who swung a broadaxe
  Was a power in the land.
We catch the gleam of greatness yet
  From those now gone to rest,
In the days of Duffy Gillis
  From the Sou-ou-West.

Then all the land was happy,
  And none were known to beg.
'Twas molasses by the puncheon
  And Jamaica by the keg;
In every home a pork-barrel,
  On every table tea,
And you couldn't find a growler
  From Decantlin's to the sea.

The pigs weighed 'leven hundred,
    The ships were on the stocks,
And everything we wanted
    We got right down at Loch's
And they charged it up against us,
    Without a fear or frown,
For they knew they'd get their money
    Whene'er the logs came down.

We did not drive in buggies then
    With horse of dubious breed,
But Concords rattled o'er our roads
    Behind the Morgan steed;
We got along at slower pace,
    For bikers weren't the rage -
If we went on a pleasant trip
    We rode in Duncan's stage.

No Scott Act then forbade us chase
    The cobwebs from our throats;
We didn't stay awake at night
    A-worrying over notes.
And all the cash we needed then
    Was carried in our vest,
For the merchant touched the button,
    And the due-bill did the rest.

We got our three square meals a day,
    And asked for nothing else,
And always had a quiet sneer
    For men who dined on smelts.
'Twas good old pork and flap-jacks,
    Swamp-soggin' if you choose,
With a Labrador for breakfast
    And two oblong Island blues.

Oh, Time! thy hand is cruel
    And the burden of thy years
Is pressing with a vengeful weight
    In sighs and doubts and fears,
And sorrow's strain is now the chord
    Where once thy music led,
And almost from the sky of life
    The bow of hope has fled.

But I'll forgive the winds of fate,
  And turn to meet the blast,
If from thy bounty thou wilt spare
  Some moments of the past.
Before you grind this discord out,
  Before you weave the shroud,
Just one more night at Colepaw's
  With the old portashin' crowd.
Where we always fed our horses,
  And put up for the night,
And gathered 'round the fireplace
  With birch logs blazing bright.
And got to swapping stories
  Till the tablecloth was spread,
When we'd all set in to supper
  And reach to for the bread.

How hunger seemed to flee before
  Those dishes boiled and fried,
With spruce beer for a chaser
  And colcannon on the side.
'Twas help yourself to stoggin'
  And cut and come again-
You couldn't pass no small dish off
  On McInerney's men.

The supper done, again we'd sit
  Around the blazing hearth,
And send the smoke wreaths curling up
  From woodstocks black as earth,
And some would read the *Gleaner*
  Before the backlog's flame,
And we'd talk Confederation
  And the wonderous "Quaybec Skame".
Then one from out the company,
  With lusty lungs and strong,
Would give out a good Come-all-ye
  'Bout ninety verses long.
Weird as a Chopin nocturn
  Came the quavers from his throat,
And every climax rounded
  By a trembling banshee note.

Then we'd pass around the bottle,
   And each man would take a swig,
And we'd welt the hardwood timbers
   While the fiddle played a jig.
When we broke into a hornpipe
   You could hear our pulses beat,
And the faster passed the bottle,
   The faster went our feet-

Till with shouts that shook the rafters
   Echoed through the Covered Bridge,
And made the snowdrifts tremble,
   On the Semiwagan Ridge,
We'd loosen up our jumpers grey,
   A deeper draught we'd take,
And 'twas "hold the light, McCarty"
   Till we make Dungarvon shake!

But gone are all the portash men,
   And gone the swampers too,
And gone the hearth at Colepaw's
   With its welcome warm and true;
And gone the good Jamaica,
   Swamp-soggin' and the rest,
And the glory is departed
   From the Sou-ou-West.

But where'er her sons are scattered,
   There still the past intrudes;
Whether in the city's maddening rush,
   Or Minnesotty's woods,
And down the glint of memory
   Like a vision from the west
Come the days of Duffy Gillis
   From the Sou-ou-West.

Glossary

Broadsheets folk poems and ballads which were printed and sold in the streets.

Bung hole is a hole filled with a stopper or cork.

Cante fable a folk narrative which includes a poem or a song. Example: "Do You Want To Buy A Cow?"

Colcannon vegetables mixed in with mashed potatoes.

Come all ye's ballads which begin with the words "Come all ye..."

Concord an open wagon.

Cookee assistant to the cook.

Deacon's bench a split log with legs on it which was used in the lumber camps in the last century.

Diddling a way of singing a tune without using words. Example: "Tee dum tee dum tee diddle de dum".

Due bill a bill of payment which could be cashed in at the company store.

Endurance rhyme jump-rope rhymes which test the skipper's endurance.

Fable tales with a moral usually using animals as the main characters. Example: "Fable of the Three Frogs".

Feu follet an Acadian term meaning "dancing lights" used to describe burning marsh gas and the Northern Lights.

Funky a lumberman who constructs logging roads.

Island blues potatoes from Prince Edward Island.

Labrador smoked herring.

Landing site near a river where logs were dumped for the spring drive.

Legend stories which reflect folk beliefs told about characters and events having their roots in history. Example: "The Old Pine Tree".

Lucifee wildcat or lynx.

Marchen wonder tales told about imaginary creatures and magical events. The hero is often an underdog who succeeds in overcoming obstacles. Example: "Three Gold Hairs From the Giant's Back".

Musquash muskrat.

Myth stories which are considered to be truthful explanations of animal traits, geological features and origins. Example: "How the Bear Got His Short Tail", "The Little People" and the Glooscap stories.

Popple poplar.

Prophetic rhymes jump-rope rhymes which are used to foretell the future. Example: "How many children will she have? One, two, three . . ."

Portashin' crowd men who brought supplies in to the lumber camps.

Quaybec Skame a proposal for Confederation discussed at the Quebec Conference in 1864.

Sawyer man employed in sawing timber.

Scott Act a prohibition law.

Shaggy-dog story stories told in a long drawn-out style using repetition, exaggeration and a humourous twist. Example: "The Ghost of the One Black Eye".

Shoepack or larrigan an ankle-length leather boot worn by lumbermen. The bottoms were sometimes dipped into molasses and oats to prevent the men from slipping on the ice.

Stoggin' filling food.

Swamp soggin' a heavy pudding made with molasses and flour.

Swampers men who cut or swamped logging roads and trails.

Tall tales humourous exaggerations. Example: "A Fishing Yarn" and "Lucky Dick".